Simply Murder
THE BATTLE OF FREDERICKSBURG

By Chris Mackowski
and Kristopher D. White

EMERGING CIVIL WAR SERIES

Savas Beatie
California

© 2012 by Chris Mackowski and Kristopher D. White

First Savas Beatie edition 2012

ISBN-13: 978-1-61121-146-7

Library of Congress Cataloging-in-Publication Data is available from the Library of Congress.

SB

Published by
Savas Beatie LLC
989 Governor Drive, Suite 102
El Dorado Hills, California 95762
Phone: 916-941-6896
Email: sales@savasbeatie.com
Web: www.savasbeatie.com

Savas Beatie titles are available at special discounts for bulk purchases in the United States by corporations, institutions, and other organizations. For more details, please contact Special Sales, P.O. Box 4527, El Dorado Hills, CA 95762, or you may e-mail us as at sales@savasbeatie.com, or visit our website at www.savasbeatie.com for additional information.

Kris: To the Fredericksburg and Spotsylvania National Military Park intern and seasonal Class of 2005.

Chris: To Mike and Ricci Jeannerette—
Mr. & Mrs. "King of the Universe"

We jointly dedicate this book to the history professors who have made a difference in our lives:
Dr. Sean Madden and Dr. Laura Tuennerman;
Bob Longnecker; and Dr. Rick Frederick—
a guy so groovy Virginia named a "burg" after him.

Touring the Battlefield

To give you a comprehensive look at the battlefield, this book deviates from the traditional National Park Service driving tour. Directions at the end of each chapter will help you follow along. At times, this tour follows the course laid out by the Park Service; at other times, it goes completely out of the park and off park lands. Important preservation work by cooperating organizations such as the Civil War Trust and the Central Virginia Battlefields Trust have saved these properties and made them available to future generations. Please support their work.

Keep in mind that some roads may have heavy traffic, and at times you will be driving in a city environment. Please follow all posted speed limits and be sure to park in designated parking areas only.

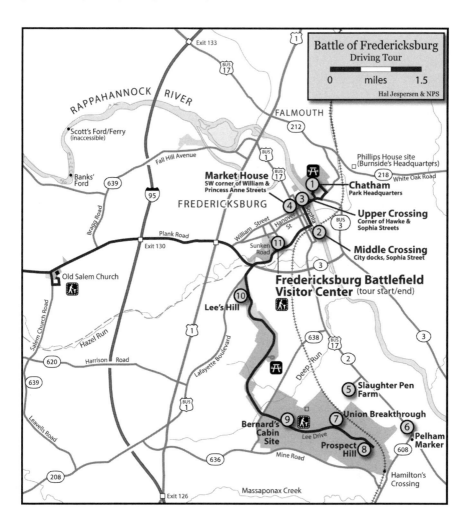

Table of Contents

List of Maps

Maps by Hal Jespersen

Acknowledgments

This book could not have been completed with out the help and support of our great friend and mentor, Frank O'Reilly. Frank is the leading expert on the Battle of Fredericksburg. Under his gracious tutelage, he took us under his wing and taught us the stories and nuances of the field. We are eternally in his debt. (Kris: Sharing an office with Frank and teaming with him on tours was a rare and great privilege.)

Thanks must be extended, too, to Don Pfanz. Don is a gentleman and scholar and has always assisted with any research request we've ever had—and honestly, he may be the single kindest person ever.

Both Frank and Don have written books on the Battle of Fredericksburg that are indispensable. *Simply Murder* is intended as a quick overview of the battle and orientation to the battlefield, but Frank and Don write with the depth and insight not possible in a slim volume like this. Their books are must-reads for any true understanding of the battle.

Greg Mertz put us both on the battlefield and continues to support our work there. We thank him for all he continues to do.

Thank you as well to Mark Allen, Tom Breen, Ray Castner, Richard Chapman, J. D. Cribbs, John Cummings, Andy Douglas, Jim Good, Gregg Kneipp, Pat Larkin, Ryan Longfellow, Fred Monner, Beth Parnicza, Jake Struhelka, and the men of the 140th Pennsylvania.

We would like to thank Kathleen Logothetis and Steward Henderson for their contributions. Logo is a fine young historian who is already doing some fascinating work, and Steward is quickly becoming a leading expert on slavery in the Fredericksburg area. We would also like to thank the other authors of *Emerging Civil War*. They are a great group of historians who allow us to bounce ideas off of them, which helps us immensely with our writing and editing.

Speaking of editing, Patrick Vecchio continues to be the most invaluable set of eyes for our work. "Mr. Bad Example" does some good, good work. We thank Heidi Hartley, Sarah White, and Caity Stuart for additional editing help. We thank Hal Jespersen for his great maps.

Finally, we extend our thanks to Savas Beatie and to editor Ted Savas. Ted's vision made the Emerging Civil War Series possible, and we're grateful for his enthusiastic support. We also appreciate the work of Sarah Keeney, who's been a treat to work with.

Chris: Thanks, too, to Pauline Hoffmann, the dean of the Russell J. Jandoli School of Journalism and Mass Communication at St. Bonaventure—an energetic and supportive boss if ever there was one. Thanks, as well, to my former NPS colleague Caity Stuart, who helped me experience and understand the Fredericksburg Battlefield in new ways. Thanks most of all to my family, especially my children, Stephanie and Jackson.

Kris: As always, this work could not have been completed without the patience and support of my family. Finally, thank you to my wife, Sarah, who loses me for weeks and months on end, holed up researching and writing. Her love and support mean everything to me. Without her support, I would not be where I am today.

Photo Credits:
Modern battlefield photography by Chris Mackowski except: Pg. 85 (snow picture) and pp. 108, 114, 134, 137 © 2011 Caity Stuart; Pg. 89 (modern canal), 133 © 2012 Kristopher White; Pp. 126 & 127 © 2012 John Cummings
Historical photos courtesy of
Fredericksburg and Spotsylvania National Military Park

What a bloody, one-sided battle this was.

It was simply murder.... We can see

when we have a chance; here we had none.

— *Union soldier*

Prologue

"Those who say they would like to visit a battlefield seldom know what they are talking about," lamented Private Erskine Church of the 27th Connecticut Infantry. "After darkness has put an end to the struggle, a hush settles over the field. Such a contrast to the roar of the fight. Never is silence more oppressive, more eloquent. You hear the cries of the wounded, which is never distinguished in the roar of battle.... You see the outlines of forms gliding through the gloom carrying on litters pale bloody men. Or perhaps your friend with his hair matted with blood over his white face and his dead eyes staring blindly up to the sky."

Church had just witnessed his first true taste of combat. He was one of the nearly 30,000 Union soldiers thrust against the now-infamous stone wall and sunken road along Marye's Heights at Fredericksburg. Thousands of dead Union soldiers dotted the 900 yards leading from the edge of the city to the Confederate position.

The charges against the stone wall ended as night settled in, cold and clear. "Shortly after we had ceased firing the cries of the wounded began to assail our ears," a soldier said. "They had lain upon the field all day and now their agonizing cries for help, broke mournfully upon the stillness of the night." An occasional cannon shot ripped through the stillness, too, and sharpshooters picked away at anything that moved.

The battle of December 13, 1862, had shaken the participants to their cores. Seven full waves of Federal infantry assaulted the famed heights, yet not a single soldier touched the wall, not one soldier made it into the road. Confederates poured an unrelenting fire at them. One Confederate claimed that he fired so many rounds, his arm was black and blue from his right elbow all the way to his right hip for the next two weeks.

Union Lt. Col. Joshua Lawrence Chamberlain of the 20th Maine spent the night of December 13 on the battlefield. The wounded cried and groaned and screamed, a cacophony "of which you could not locate the source..." he later recalled, "a wail so far and deep and wide, as if a thousand discords were flowing together into a key-note weird, unearthly, terrible to hear and bear."

Artillery poured from the crest of the heights. Federals had to cross uphill over a clear field of fire, and Confederates used these fields, coupled with strategic high points, to converge artillery from three different points down onto the approaching Yankees.

The casualties were horrific. Nearly one in three Union soldiers who ventured toward the heights became a casualty.

Now, with thousands of men caught between the lines, the night of December 13th was a nightmare for the men of both sides.

"When night descended upon the bloody field nearly 1,500 dead soldiers lay upon an area of two acres in front of our lines," wrote Confederate James Hagood. "Three or four times as many wounded howled in the darkness a dismal concert for assistance which could not be rendered, or perished in the cold from neglect. The pickets of the enemy's army which were posted that night on the skirts of town erected breastworks of the dead bodies and thus secured themselves from the bullets of the Confederate Sharpshooters."

"What a sight!" a Union soldier recalled. "To see men by the thousands lying in such a position covered or protected by a slight rise of ground…that rise furnishing the only barrier between themselves and death. It fairly made my heart sick."

Any Union soldier who attempted to escape the horrors of the field had to run a gauntlet of sniper fire. Those who chose to stay—and most did because the clear night offered the snipers plenty of light for carrying out their work—had to endure temperatures that sank to a nighttime low of 40. The thermometer had reached 56 degrees earlier in the day, prompting many of the Federals to leave their heavy winter coats back in camp or shed them as they advanced through the city. Now the men in the muddied fields and damp uniforms nearly froze to the ground.

The living were mixed with the dead. "One poor fellow's dead body lay within three feet of me all day, the whole top of his head carried off by a shell, the eyes were open and stared at me whenever I looked at him," said Sergeant Thomas Bowen of the 12th U.S. Infantry. "When it came dark I rolled him over so he could not look at me…."

One New Hampshire regiment attempted to find their comrades' bodies in the dark. Because they could not use lanterns, they had to feel dead men's faces to identify them.

Those not seeking comrades did what they could to protect themselves from the enemy and the cold. The 22nd Massachusetts passed the night in the latrines—the "sinks," they called them. The smell was ungodly but the protection of their improvised "earthwork" helped keep many of the Bay Staters safe.

One staff officer pulled out his blanket and curled up on a

Confederate commander Gen. Robert E. Lee. Watching the spectacle of war unfold before him from his headquarters on Telegraph Hill, Lee said, "It is a good thing war is so terrible, or we should grow too fond of it."

manure pile. The heat from the pile at least offered the officer some warmth.

In town, Union field hospitals had to cover their windows and keep their doors shut as much as possible. Otherwise, when light escaped, Confederates fired artillery at it. There were so many Union soldiers in the city that many men were forced to sleep on the sidewalks or even in the streets themselves.

What had gone so wrong? How did the Army of the Potomac, the most famous army fighting for the Union cause, come to such a horrific and lopsided defeat? Did they ever stand a chance to win on this field? Was the assault a forlorn hope from the start?

"Those who say they would like to visit a battlefield seldom know what they are talking about...."

The Campaign

CHAPTER ONE

"[W]ar is not merely a political act," wrote the Prussian military theorist Carl Von Clausewitz, "but also a real political instrument, a continuation of political commerce, a carrying out of the same by other means." Few campaigns in the Civil War embody this idea better than the one that led to Fredericksburg.

The battle of Fredericksburg, fought Dec. 11-13, 1862, is widely viewed as Union Major General Ambrose Burnside's greatest blunder. Many also view it as one of the greatest blunders in American military history. While the battle was indeed a debacle for the Army of the Potomac, and it was likewise an unnecessary waste of time, men, and material, the blame should not fall solely at the feet of Ambrose Burnside. Although Burnside was the commander on the field, it was the political will of President Abraham Lincoln and his administration that forced Burnside into action.

The roots of the campaign lay in the fertile fields of Sharpsburg, Maryland. On September 17, 1862, the armies clashed in the battle of Antietam, America's bloodiest single day. Across cornfields and arched bridges, the Army of the Potomac grappled with the Army of Northern Virginia, ending the day in stalemate. The timid and overly cautious Union commander, Major General George McClellan, outnumbered and outgunned General Robert E. Lee's weaker Southern army by nearly two-to-one. Still, McClellan could not land the fatal blow. On September 19, the Confederate army slipped away into Virginia. Only after Lee's men had safely withdrawn to the south side of the Potomac River did McClellan timidly probe and slowly pursue the old gray fox.

Rohrbach Bridge across Antietam Creek now bears Burnside's name. The Fredericksburg campaign grew from seeds planted here in Maryland following the Battle of Antietam in September 1862.

However, because Lee left McClellan in control of the field, McClellan and Lincoln claimed Antietam as a victory. As a result, on September 22, 1862, Lincoln issued the preliminary Emancipation Proclamation. In reality, the Proclamation had no teeth because it freed slaves only in areas of rebellion, so

Before meeting on the banks of the Rappahannock River in December, the armies met in September on the banks of Antietam Creek. There, Confederates used a sunken road as a fortified rifle pit to resist Federal assaults; once Federals broke through, they inflicted heavy casualties. At Fredericksburg, Confederates again used a sunken road as a fortified rifle pit to resist Federal assaults—with a much different result.

there was no way to actually enforce it except through military victory. Nonetheless, as a symbolic gesture, it pleased many abolitionists and enraged the South. "If I am remembered in history," Lincoln would say, "it will be for this."

Lincoln planned to sign the official Emancipation Proclamation on January 1, 1863. In the months leading to that, Lincoln urged Union commanders to go on the offensive. He needed battlefield victories to give the Proclamation credibility. Unfortunately for Lincoln, those victories would be few and far between.

By late October 1862, it was clear to Lincoln that McClellan was not the man to lead the Army of the Potomac to any such victories. The proud and popular McClellan was a darling of the Democrats, though, and with midterm elections coming up, Lincoln, a Republican, couldn't risk upsetting the political climate any worse than it already was. Not until November 7, the day after the elections, did Lincoln make a change: He removed the beloved but slothful McClellan from command and replaced him with McClellan's close friend, Ambrose Burnside.

Burnside was an 1847 graduate of the United States Military Academy at West Point and a veteran of the old army, but he had been a failure as an antebellum businessman. After civil war broke out, Burnside headed a brigade at First Manassas and led aggressive amphibious operations against the North Carolina Coast—exploits that won him

Union Maj. Gen. Ambrose E. Burnside

Despite his lackluster performance at Antietam, Burnside had a reputation as a fighter because of his successes in early 1862 along the North Carolina coast.

wide acclaim. He had commanded, for a time, a wing of McClellan's army during the Antietam campaign, but he was best known as the commander of Ninth Army Corps. Lincoln hoped Burnside possessed a fire that McClellan lacked.

The army itself had its doubts. "The news struck like an electric shock," wrote a captain in the Sixth Corps. "Every man is discouraged and the heart of the army is broken."

None moreso than Burnside, who took the assignment out of obligation even as he voiced reservations about his own abilities. "I am not fit for it," he had told General-in-Chief Major General Henry Halleck. "There are many more in the army better fitted than I am; but if you and the President insist, I will take it and do the best I can." Union Major General William B. Franklin noted Burnside's "utter demoralization…on the first morning after his assumption to command, his entire loss of face & will, & the unstrung condition of his nerves…."

Burnside met with his old friend McClellan, who briefed him on the army's dispositions and outlined an offensive he had conjured up but had not yet set into motion. After three days of meetings and goodbyes, McClellan left the Army of the Potomac for the final time.

"The army takes the new change kindly enough," Union Brigadier General Orlando Willcox wrote. "Although I think that the general opinion is that it hardly does justice to either general, relieving one while succeeding & putting the other in his shoes to take up his plans, substantially without having time to form new or different ones of his own."

Aside from some supply problems McClellan had warned him about, Burnside took the reins of an army in better condition and better spirits than it had been even before its fight at Antietam. Since the battle, McClellan had given

"Burnside is a pure man and a man of integrity of purpose," Maj. Gen. George McClellan said as he took his leave of the army following his removal from command, "and such a man can't go far astray."

the army plenty of rest, positioning it around Warrenton, Virginia, to watch Lee's army and protect Washington from a Confederate offensive that was not forthcoming. Manpower had increased to over 123,000 men, much of it attributed to an influx of nine-month regiments during and following the invasion of the North—the "Crisis of 1862."

Burnside set off to meet with Lincoln and Halleck. Derisively nicknamed "Old Brains," Halleck's overcautious, meddlesome nature, and his never-ending efforts to cover his own backside, cost many an officer his job—and in this case, would help cost Burnside the campaign.

Burnside laid out a plan to draw Lee's army into a fight by threatening Richmond. Speed was the key to the plan for two major reasons: First, the weather could change from fall to winter at any moment; and second, Lincoln wanted a victory before January 1, 1863, when the final Proclamation would go into effect. The Union commander felt the fastest way to Richmond would be through Fredericksburg.

Burnside did not intend to fight there, though. Instead, he hoped to swing three-quarters of his army south of the city to seize the Richmond, Fredericksburg and Potomac Railroad (RF&P); the Telegraph Road (known today as the Sunken Road); and the Richmond Highway (also known then as the Bowling Green Road). He could then move his army toward Richmond along the parallel roads while using the RF&P to keep it well supplied.

There was a major problem with Burnside's plan, however. The three bridges spanning the Rappahannock—the Falmouth Bridge, the William Street Bridge (also known as the Chatham Bridge), and the Railroad Bridge—had all been

Union General-in-Chief Henry Halleck, known as "Old Brains"

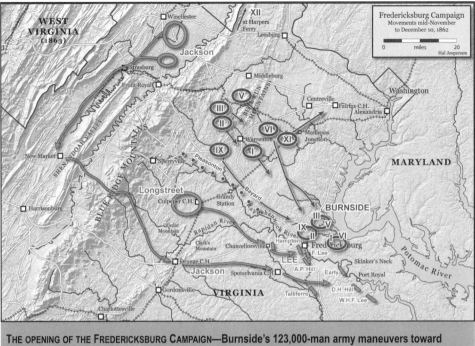

THE OPENING OF THE FREDERICKSBURG CAMPAIGN—Burnside's 123,000-man army maneuvers toward the city of Fredericksburg with the intent to cross and drive south toward the Confederate capital of Richmond. Lee's 78,000 men move from the Shenandoah Valley to block Burnside's direct route.

destroyed by the Confederates in the spring of 1862. Burnside knew this, though, and before embarking on the campaign made preparations with Halleck to have temporary pontoon bridges awaiting the army's arrival at Fredericksburg.

On November 14, Lincoln green-lighted Burnside's campaign. Halleck urged his subordinate to move quickly, and Burnside had his army on the road on November 15.

Rain showers and muddy roads swamped the army's march toward Fredericksburg, but Burnside's men still traversed the forty or so miles in just two days. "On! on! on! we went rapidly and without a single rest!" wrote a Pennsylvania private. "Sometimes we almost stopped, and we began to hope that we would ease our aching shoulders of their burdens, but soon we had to compensate for our slowness by going almost on a run! Never were we used so hard before!"

Around them, soldiers saw the toll of war on the landscape. "The country between this and Warrenton is the most forlorn looking I ever beheld," a Pennsylvanian wrote. "Not one acre in a thousand is under cultivation. I saw but one small field of grain on the way. The people of the community must starve if they depend on what they produce. You cannot imagine a country or people so destitute as this."

By November 17, the lead elements of Major General Darius Couch's 2nd Corps were overlooking the city from

Pontoons measured thirty feet long and each one weighed nearly a ton. They had to be transported overland via their own wagons strung together in long trains.

the northern and western bank of the Rappahannock River. Fewer than 1,000 Confederates occupied the area in and around Fredericksburg. Burnside needed only to construct the pontoon bridges, and he could cross the river and make his dash toward Richmond—but it was not to be. Halleck had neglected to issue the necessary orders to move the bridging materials toward Fredericksburg. In fact, he didn't issue them until November 17, the day Burnside's men arrived.

Moving the bridges from Harper's Ferry, Virginia (modern-day West Virginia), and Berlin, Maryland, was a comedy of errors. Not only had Halleck's orders come far too late, but there were not enough specialized wagons to carry the boats. Once Federal engineers did have the wagons, they then had four hundred unbroken mules to deal with. Some engineers tried to strap the boats together in the form of a small barge and float the boats down the Potomac River, but the barges ran aground on sandbars because of low tides.

Ten days after Burnside's army arrived in Fredericksburg, his bridging materials arrived, too.

During those same ten days, Confederates began to appear in force. Burnside's speedy movement had caught Lee off guard, and he initially looked to defend the North Anna River, twenty-five miles south of Fredericksburg. Once Lee realized his foe was stuck, though, he dispatched Lieutenant General James Longstreet, with his 40,000-man First Corps, from the Culpeper area to Fredericksburg.

"A grand exodus is going on," a Confederate noted as the First Corps approached the city; "all day long we met people, old and young, leaving the city, carrying their household goods with them. Carts and wagons containing their bedding, etc., going to the rear. Children and women all in the procession."

Longstreet initially hid behind Marye's Heights but eventually showed himself. His men held the Telegraph Road, and Longstreet's cannon commanded the city, railroad, and Bowling Green Road.

Burnside's most direct route to Richmond was blocked.

Confederate Lt. Gen. James Longstreet, Lee's "Old Warhorse"

Fredericksburg as seen from the Federal side of the river. Abutments for two of the destroyed bridges remained standing in the river.

At the Visitor Center

The battle for Marye's Heights and the Sunken Road is the best-known portion of the Battle of Fredericksburg, but the full story of the battle is far more complex. Therefore, we'll travel to other important areas of the battlefield, eventually ending here where we started.

Before you begin the tour, you may want to stop in the visitor center. An orientation film and exhibits on the battle will acquaint you with the sites and stories you are about to see and read. Restrooms are also available.

The Civilian Conservation Corps built the visitor center in 1936 to replace a small contact station that sat across the street. At the time of the battle, a home sat roughly on the spot where the visitor center now stands: the Hall House, a two-story wooden structure so riddled with bullet and shell damage that it had to be torn down after the war.

→ TO STOP 1

From the visitor center parking lot, turn left onto Lafayette Boulevard and drive 0.8 miles to the T-intersection at Sophia Street. At the stop sign, turn left and follow Sophia Street 0.4 miles to William Street. At the traffic light at William Street, turn right and cross the Chatham Bridge. Follow William Street/King's Highway 0.3 miles to a traffic light, where you will turn left onto Chatham Heights Road. Follow Chatham Heights Road for 0.1 miles and turn left onto Chatham Lane. A brown Park Service sign will point the way. Follow Chatham Lane to the parking area. On the Park Service's driving tour, this is tour stop one, "Chatham."

GPS Coordinates: N 38° 30911 W 77° 45418

The Battlefield Visitor Center in its early days.

Chatham

CHAPTER TWO

In the ten days it took for the Federal pontoon bridges to reach the front, Ambrose Burnside did not sit idly by. He and his men scouted up and down the Rappahannock River for possible crossing points. Upriver, the Rappahannock offered many fordable points, but Southern horsemen and infantry picketed most of them. Burnside also worried that if he forded the river before the bridges arrived, rain and snow might swell the river, stranding portions of his army on the Confederate side and making them easy targets for his adversary.

Downriver, Burnside looked at crossing at Port Royal, Virginia. A crossing there would offer access to roads leading to the Confederate capital, but shifting his army another thirty miles in that direction would extend his supply lines uncomfortably, and he would still be subject to nature's whims and the keen eyes of Southern patrols. Lee, meanwhile, could easily shift the bulk of his army downriver to block the Federal move. "It appears to me that should General Burnside change his base of operations, the effect produced in the United States would be almost equivalent to a defeat," Lee wrote to Confederate President Jefferson Davis. "I think, therefore, he will persevere in his present course, and the longer we can delay him, and throw him into the winter, the more difficult will be his undertaking."

But Burnside couldn't wait for winter. With the final Emancipation Proclamation due January 1, Lincoln demanded action. "Burnside was compelled by the force of public will—if nothing more—to make the attempt at all hazards & against every obstacle," explained one of his subordinates.

Thus pressured, Burnside proposed to cross at Fredericksburg itself. "I think now that the enemy will be more surprised by a crossing in our immediate front than any other part of the river," he said.

Burnside would use his engineers—specialized construction troops—to roll bridging material to the riverfront opposite the

Chatham, a Georgian-style mansion built atop Stafford Heights across the river from Fredericksburg, dates back to the city's colonial period.

The delayed movement of pontoons from Maryland to Fredericksburg left Burnside's army high and dry.

The Park Service has model pontoons, built to two-thirds scale, on display at Chatham. They sit on the terraced lawn facing the Rappahannock.

north and south ends of the city, roughly one mile from each other. Federal soldiers crossing at those two points would seize control of the town and hold the attention of Lee's men perched on Marye's Heights.

Meanwhile, further downriver, a little over a mile south of the city on a portion of the river known as "The Bend" (known today as Franklin's Crossing), engineers would construct a third bridge site. Federals would cross into an open country of vast rolling fields and approach two of their main objectives: the Bowling Green Road; and the Richmond, Fredericksburg and Potomac Railroad. Maneuvering on this portion of the battlefield would be much easier for Union soldiers, too, since they would not have to deal with the cramped confines of city streets.

Burnside planned to execute the crossing as quickly as possible. Engineers could get a pre-dawn start, and by mid-afternoon the bulk of the Union army could move across the bridges. It could all be done in less than a day, leaving plenty of time in the afternoon and evening to finalize preparations for an assault against the enemy the next morning. That attack, also planned for a pre-dawn launch, would hit the Confederate line at opposite ends of the field.

The main Federal thrust would be aimed toward a small rise of ground five miles to the south of the city known by the locals as Prospect Hill. Burnside intended to launch nearly 65,000 Union men toward the hill in an effort to push the Confederates to the west and north, away from the Bowling Green Road and away from Richmond. While that happened, a heavy reserve of troops would then move along the Bowling Green Road toward the Confederate capital. Burnside looked to pry the door open and pour Federal soldiers in.

Simultaneously, the north sector in front of Marye's

Heights would also come alive. Union soldiers, nearly 30,000 in all, would march out of the city and attack the heights. If they broke through, their success would be a marvelous flourish to Burnside's plan, but realistically, the men were expected only to hold Confederates there in place so that they could not shift south and reinforce Prospect Hill when it came under attack.

On paper, the plan looked solid. In execution, it would begin to unravel almost immediately.

*   *   *

From Falmouth, where the Rappahannock makes its wide turn southward, a series of ridges known as Stafford Heights runs along the river's western bank. "These hills rise high above the river, commanding an extensive view from their summit, of the surrounding country, and the city of Fredericksburg on the opposite shore," a Confederate later wrote. "The sides of these hills, above Falmouth, were dotted here and there with woods from their top to the water's edge, while below the town, they presented to the eye, a barren, bleak appearance, destitute of vegetation of any kind."

In between those tree-dotted hills and the barren lands sat the stately plantation home called Chatham, named for British Prime Minister William Pitt, the First Earl of Chatham. The

The lower crossing site near "The Bend" would eventually be known as Franklin's Crossing, named after the Union general charged with crossing the river there.

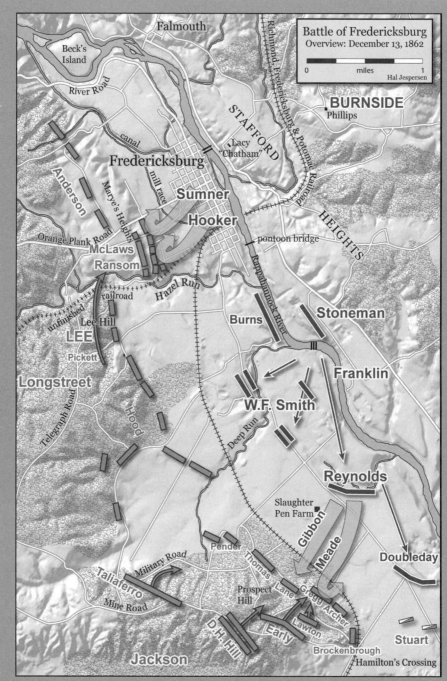

THE BATTLE OF FREDERICKSBURG—Burnside's plan called for assaults on two portions of the Confederate line. The main assault would take place south of the city, targeting Prospect Hill. The second assault would emerge from the western side of the city and strike the Confederate line at Marye's Heights. Leading up to the battle, the Confederate southern flank was stretched over a twenty-five-mile front, so Burnside's plan would have had him attacking the weakest part of the Southern position. Federal delays, however, gave Confederates time to consolidate.

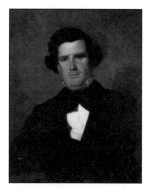

The river-facing side of Chatham once boasted a columned porch. Traces of the columns can still be seen on the facade today.

house was constructed between 1768 and 1771 by William Fitzhugh, a wealthy landowner with many connections in pre-Revolutionary Virginia. To build his mansion, Fitzhugh sold 10,000 acres of his land holdings in Virginia. He employed a cadre of skilled artisans, craftsman, and slaves to build the Georgian-style mansion, made entirely of brick, two stories high plus a full basement. When work finished on the home in the autumn of 1771, Fitzhugh and his pregnant wife, Nancy, moved in. In November, their daughter Lucy was born.

Fitzhugh's estate touched the banks of the Rappahannock at the base of the heights and ran east and north from the river, totaling nearly 1,280 acres. "That elegant and highly improved seat," as it was hailed, was the envy of many a Fredericksburg resident. The plantation consisted of the main house and an icehouse, dairy, kitchen, barns, and stables. Fitzhugh was also an avid admirer of horses, and he loved gambling, so he built a racetrack.

James Horace Lacy, whom one Federal officer referred to as "the most dangerous man in the Confederacy" because of his wealth, connections, and fiery anti-Union passions.

Fitzhugh served in the Virginia House of Burgesses and had many powerful friends in the colonies, and they visited Chatham frequently, often staying several weeks at a time. Among Fitzhugh's visitors at various times: George Washington, Thomas Jefferson, James Madison, and James Monroe.

Eventually, the financial burden of entertaining forced Fitzhugh to close up his home in 1796 and move to Alexandria. The home didn't sell until May of 1806—bought then by Major Churchill Jones, formerly of the Continental army, for $20,000. The home stayed in the Jones family for sixty-six years.

By the outbreak of the Civil War, Chatham was owned by James Horace Lacy—one of two plantation homes he owned in the Fredericksburg area (Ellwood, seventeen miles to the west, was the other). Lacy had installed terraced gardens on

What today serves as the back side of Chatham was once the 18th and 19th century front of the home. Carriages came up a drive that deposited visitors at the front porch.

the Fredericksburg side of the home, as well as a porch with large wooden pillars.

During the first Federal occupation of the city in the spring of 1862, Brigadier General Rufus King took Lacy's home for his headquarters. President Lincoln met there with members of his cabinet as well as General Irvin McDowell. The famed Iron Brigade camped on the grounds, in what is today Pratt Park, less than a mile from the home. Those Federals had all left the area well before the opening of the winter campaign—but now they were back.

As the Army of the Potomac settled in along the north and west bank of the Rappahannock, Burnside set his headquarters up at the Phillips House, about a mile east of Chatham, while his second-in-command, Major General Edwin Voss Sumner, settled into Chatham itself. Known as "Bull," Sumner's nickname came in part from his great booming voice. It originated, too, from an incident years earlier in the Mexican War, where a musket ball struck him in the head and glanced off without penetrating his "bullheaded" skull.

Aside from its use as Sumner's headquarters, Chatham was used as a Federal hospital. Tents for the sick and wounded lined the area where the garden sits today. Beyond, in a large field adjacent to the modern parking lot, Major General Darius Couch's Union 2nd Corps encamped, and when engineers finally arrived with the pontoons, the big flat-bottomed boats were parked in the area as well. Ravines to the north and south of the house would provide ready avenues to the river when the time came to get the pontoons into position. Federals also established a signal post for communications outside the house.

Union Maj. Gen. Edwin "Bull" Sumner

The Phillips House,
Burnside's headquarters.

To the north and south of Chatham, artillery lined the crest of Stafford Heights—some 147 to start with, 183 total, arrayed by Brigadier General Henry Hunt, Burnside's chief of artillery. From there, his imposing long guns could cover the city of Fredericksburg and the vast open fields to the south and west of the city. The long arm of Burnside's army could extend its touch to any point along the seven-mile Confederate line, from Marye's Heights to Howison Hill and all the way down to Prospect Hill. Even Lee's Headquarters on Telegraph Hill fell within easy range.

"We have been here a week now looking at the rebles [sic] like two bull-dogs neither one daring to bark," wrote an antsy Rhode Islander to his sister.

Four weeks would pass in all before Burnside finally mobilized his army. He passed down orders on the evening of December 10. The next great battle of the war was about to begin.

At Chatham

The Union Army used Chatham on a number of occasions, for a variety of purposes: a headquarters, picket post, and a stable. On two separate occasions, Chatham served as a Union hospital. Wounded soldiers lined the floors through most of the downstairs, and many scratched their names and units into the wooden trim inside the house and out.

The north wing—the right end of the home as you approach from the parking lot—served as an operating room. "Outdoors, at the foot of a tree, within ten yards of the front of the house," recalled Walt Whitman, likely referring to a still-standing Catalpa tree, "I noticed a heap of amputated feet, legs, arms, hands, etc.—about a load for a one-horse cart. Several dead bodies lie near, each covered with its brown woolen blanket. In the dooryard, toward the river, are fresh graves, mostly of officers, their names on pieces of barrel staves or broken board, stuck in the dirt." Whitman, along

The catalpa tree behind
Chatham is a witness tree.

"Outdoors,
at the foot of a tree,
within ten yards of
the front of the house,
I noticed a heap of
amputated feet, legs,
arms, hands, etc.
—about a load for
a one-horse cart."

— Walt Whitman

with Clara Barton and Dr. Mary Walker, were among those who tended to the wounded on Chatham's grounds.

One-hundred thirty soldiers were initially buried on Chatham's grounds. All but three were exhumed and interred at the Fredericksburg National Cemetery on Marye's Heights. The three who remain were not located until after the cemetery had closed to new interments.

The hard hand of war left a lasting impact on the once-grand estate. The financially strapped J. Horace Lacy, once labeled "the most dangerous Rebel in the county" by Major General Abner Doubleday, was forced to sell the home in 1872. The loss of much of his fortune, coupled with the wartime damage, was too much for Lacy to bear financially. After that, the estate went through a number of ownership changes, and the grounds and façade morphed with each new owner. The house was "reoriented"—the front became the back. The porches and porticos were removed. Elaborate gardens sprung up.

Once 1,300 acres, the Chatham estate dwindled over time to just over eighty acres. Today, the 12,000-square-foot mansion houses a museum, an orientation film, and the park's administrative offices.

The grave of one of the unknown soldiers still buried on Chatham's grounds.

→ TO STOP 2

Turn right onto the gravel driveway that leads around the front of Chatham. Once at the end of the gravel driveway, bear left onto River Road. *Be careful turning onto this road because oncoming traffic tends to speed.* At the stop sign, turn right and cross the Chatham Bridge 0.2 miles. At the end of the bridge, turn left onto Sophia Street and follow it 0.6 miles to its terminus at the City Dock.

GPS Coordinates: N 38° 29679 W 77° 77.45317

Helen and Daniel Devore planted Chatham's lush gardens in the 1920s. Later, the large brick wall was installed by the home's last private owner, John Lee Pratt.

Seige guns face the river from Chatham's terraces.

The Middle Crossing

CHAPTER THREE

As the Union army sat and waited, it proved too tempting a target to resist—not for Confederate soldiers but for a number of civilians who took up arms to defend their home town. Fredericksburg housed bushwhackers and sharpshooters of all sorts who fired on the east bank of the Rappahannock, harassing the troops of Darius Couch's Second Corps. It became such an issue that Sumner, commander of the Right Grand Division, sent the provost marshal of the army, Brigadier General Marsena Patrick, across the river with a warning. Described as "the finest existing fossil of the Cenozoic age," Patrick was not a man to provoke, and his order from Sumner suggested that he meant business:

Dated November 21st, 1862.

To the Mayor and Common Council of Fredericksburg. Gentlemen: Under cover of the houses of your city, shots have been fired upon the troops of my command. Your mills and manufactories are furnishing provisions and material for the clothing for armed bodies in rebellion against the Government of the United States. Your railroads and other means of transportation are removing supplies to the depots of such troops. This condition of things must terminate, and by direction of General Burnside I accordingly demand the surrender of your city into my hands, as the representative of the Government of the United States, at or before 5 o'clock this afternoon. Failing in an affirmative reply to this demand by the hour indicated, sixteen hours will be permitted to elapse for the removal from the city of women and children, the sick and wounded and aged, etc., which period having expired I shall proceed to shell the town. Upon obtaining possession of the city every necessary means will be taken to preserve the order and secure the protective operation of the laws and policy of the United States Government.

I am, very respectfully, your obedient servant, E. V. Sumner

During the December battle, Union men crossed the Rappahannock on a single 420-foot pontoon bridge, then used Rocky Lane— the original road leading to the ferry and docks—to enter the lower end of the city. In February 2006, after a six-week project, the road was brought back to its historical appearance.

Residents began to evacuate the city when Burnside's army appeared on the far bank. "[A] sad sight it is," a Confederate soldier wrote.

Under other conditions, the city council and Mayor Montgomery Slaughter would have quickly caved to Sumner's demands, but on November 20, Longstreet's lead elements had arrived. Rather than surrender, city officials, in consultation with Lee's Old Warhorse, chose to evacuate women and children from the city. Though the Union dander was up, Federals were still level headed enough to leave the citizenry alone. Patrick went so far as to say the city would not be shelled unless "she fires"—placing the proverbial cannon ball squarely in Lee's court. If the Confederate commander intended to defend the city or use it as a shield, the Union army would only respect the private property of its citizens until the first shot was fired.

Confederate soldier Charles Minor Blackford witnessed the evacuation:

I rode into Fredericksburg and a sad sight it is. The people, as far as possible, are all leaving and are carrying away everything they can possibly get off. A large detail of wagons and ambulances is sent into town every day to help them move, and it is amusing to see the soldiers help them. As far as I have heard any expression of opinion the citizens generally prefer the place be burnt to the ground rather than it should be surrendered to the Yankees.

As citizens left, Confederate infantry arrived: Brigadier General William Barksdale's all-Mississippi Brigade deployed in the houses, warehouses, and factories along the riverfront. They dug trenches and set up roadblocks in the area, too, then set to learning the city streets they'd been tasked to defend. Barksdale, a firebrand politician-turned-solider, set his headquarters up in the City Market House on Princess Anne Street and then Barksdale commenced to waiting.

Brig. Gen. Marsena Patrick

*   *   *

Twenty-four degrees, one thermostat read.

2:00 a.m., December 11.

Moving quietly, men of the 15th New York Engineers moved their pontoon trains to the river's edge opposite the south end of the city. Their job was to lay a single bridge that would span 420 feet of river. According to some of the men, a thin layer of ice covered much of the river, which worried them: they feared the ice would creek and crack as they placed boats in the water and give away their position. They at least had the cover of a heavy fog, rising from open stretches of the river, to cloak their work.

Brig. Gen. William Barksdale

As the engineers set to it, members of the 46th and 89th New York Infantry lined the bank to provide fire support and extra muscle if the bridge-builders needed it. Work went apace unmolested.

But at 5:00 a.m., with the bridges more than halfway across the river, a pair of Confederate cannon broke the predawn quiet. Although not aimed at the engineers, the guns could not have had a more devastating effect: they signaled Lee's men to mobilize for action. Fearing the worst, the Federal engineers picked up their pace, nearly frenzied in their work, desperately trying to balance speed with silence. Ten more minutes passed. Then, the morning quiet broke again, this time with scattered rifle shots from Mississippians concealed in the warehouses along the far riverbank.

"Barksdale's men had reported, early in the night, the noise of boats & material being unloaded on the enemy's side, & long before daylight they could hear boats being put in the water & work commenced," a Confederate artillerist later reported. "But they were ordered to let the enemy get well committed to his work & to wait for good daylight before opening fire."

An artist's rendition of Union Engineers as they attempt to bridge the river under fire.

The site of the middle crossing, across from the Fredericksburg city docks.

Confederate sharpshooters hunkered down in the city.

The engineers—in the river, in boats, and on the bridges—made enticing targets. As Confederates picked them off, the engineers abandoned their bridge and ran for cover on the Federal shore. The infantry support there, meanwhile, fired blindly across the river, doing little to dislodge their Southern counterparts. Confederates, clustered in small groups, two to twenty per building, could simply duck and hide when the Federal volleys rang out.

When the firing died down, a lull settled over the river. Out crept the engineers. No sooner did they again set to work on the bridge than Barksdale's Mississippians set to work on them. The engineers scurried for safety, the New Yorkers fired volley after volley, the Mississippians ducked under cover. The cat-and-mouse stretched on for hours.

The delay infuriated Burnside. "The army is held by the throat by a few sharpshooters!" he fumed. To break the stalemate, he ordered Hunt, his chief of artillery, to use the 147 cannon atop Stafford Heights to drive out the sharpshooters. Now that Lee had broken his promise not to use the city for military purposes, Burnside felt no compunction about breaking his promise not to bombard the city. The guns bucked to life.

"When the artillery fairly opened the roar was terrific—dreadful—I know of no words to express it," claimed Surgeon Clark Baum of the 50th New York Engineers. "The screeching of the shells thru the air the whiz of the solid shot, the boom boom, boom of the cannon, the sharp ring of the rifles and rattle of the musketry all commingled made one's ears tingle."

Union artillery lined up on Stafford Heights.

Union batteries fired one round every three minutes into the city. The ground shook. Shells burst in the air. Buildings fell in on the Rebels.

"Tons of iron were hurled against this place," one Mississippian recalled. "[T]he deafening roar of cannon and bursting shells, falling walls and chimneys, bricks and timbers flying through the air, houses set on fire, the smoke adding to the already heavy fog, the bursting flames through the housetops, made a scene which has no parallel in history. It was appalling and indescribable, a condition which would paralyze the stoutest heart, and one from which not a man in Barksdale's Brigade had the slightest hope of escaping."

But they didn't need to escape; they needed only to sit tight and wait for the storm to exhaust itself. Hunt's artillery could not drive them out, as well-ensconced as they were. At best, Hunt could prevent reinforcements from moving in, but he couldn't stop the Mississippians from firing on the engineers every time the engineers tried to resume work. Hunt's artillery even helped the Confederates in a way: many of the houses Barksdale's men holed up in were made of wood, so when a percussion shell hit, instead of detonating it often punched a large hole right through the building. The Confederates protected in the house had yet one more portal from which to fire.

The weather had also dampened Union munitions. In the mornings, temperatures had dropped below freezing, but in the afternoons temperature rose into the fifties and sixties. Frequent rain and snow compounded the problem. Many timed fuses simply wouldn't detonate because the powder in the shells had become damp.

If Lee "wants a bridge of dead Yankees," Barksdale said confidently, "[I] can furnish him with one."

By mid-afternoon, with little to no progress made on the bridge, Hunt decided to try another tack. With so many yet-unused pontoon boats, plenty were available to use for

Brig. Gen. Henry Hunt

As Federal troops established a bridgehead, reinforcements continued to ferry across.

transporting infantry to the far side of the river. There, they could establish a beachhead and, block by block if necessary, drive the Confederates out of the town. Hunt's idea, novel at the time, would be the first riverine crossing under fire in American military history.

While it seems today like common sense to put soldiers in a boat to row them across a river for an attack, it had never before been done in American military history.

Men of the 89th New York were "voluntold" that they would cross the river. Near 3:00 p.m., the Empire State men piled into boats and crossed. The pontoons, with square bows built for stability, not speed, turtled across the river while Confederates fired fast and furious. However, once the New Yorkers made it just past the halfway mark of the river, the Confederate fire slackened, then stopped altogether. Men in the warehouses couldn't see over the crest of the riverbank to fire any more. Meanwhile, the men in the houses on the bluffs couldn't see past the roofs of the warehouses (today, level open ground where the parking lot sits).

Once the pontoons reached the shore, the New Yorkers leapt from the boats and cleared the riverfront as quickly as possible. At the same time, the engineers set back to their bridge-building. Within a half an hour, they completed their span. Blue columns began to file across immediately.

The Middle Crossing, as it became known, was now secure—but on the north end of town a bloody battle was shaping up at the Upper Crossing.

At The Middle Crossing

Being the northernmost navigable point on the Rappahannock River brought a great deal of commerce in and out of the city of Fredericksburg. Farmers and merchants from surrounding communities brought their wares to the port, where it made its way down the tidal river to the Chesapeake Bay, where most ships turned north and docked in Baltimore, Maryland—Fredericksburg's sister city.

Here along the riverfront stood warehouses and a mill. With your back to Sophia Street, a look down along the green expanse on the Fredericksburg side of the river shows indications of deep depressions left by warehouse foundations.

Stafford Heights rises on the far side of the river. On the cleared hillside, diagonal from the modern boat launch, sits George Washington's Ferry Farm, his boyhood home. In the days before bridges spanned the Rappahannock, the Washingtons operated a rope ferry. Here, too, was the supposed site where young George attempted to throw a silver dollar across the river.

Recessed in the parking island at the city docks is a small monument commemorating the actions of the famed Irish Brigade. Dedicated on December 15, 1998, the monument cost $4,000; three Civil War reenacting groups raised the funds.

The Washington family ferry was long gone by the time of the Civil War, but this area still made an excellent crossing point. In May 1862, a makeshift bridge was constructed of canal boats, and President Lincoln crossed the rickety span to visit the then-occupied city.

At one time, a monument stood on the east side of Sophia Street to mark the Middle Crossing site. Dedicated in December 1917 by the United Daughters of the Confederacy, it disappeared by 1923, most likely washed away in one of the many floods that have swept this area.

⟶ TO STOP 3

From the parking area, follow Sophia Street 0.8 miles. Turn left onto Fauquier Street and park on the side of the road. Exit your vehicle and walk back to Sophia Street. Turn left and follow Sophia Street one block. The Upper Crossing is on your right, at the foot of Hawke Street.

GPS Coordinates: N 38° .30697 W 77° 77.46051

The Upper Crossing

CHAPTER FOUR

"I went out just as the first of a long pontoon train moved silently down the hill, and slid one boat after another into the river," wrote a Pennsylvania sergeant who'd been going out for picket duty near Chatham. It was around 2:00 a.m. on December 11. "Straw had been scattered and tan bark placed on all rough spots, it was wonderful how these huge loads could pass close by us and, although we could see them in the darkness, not a sound or rattle was made."

Some engineers broke the stillness when they decided to take pontoons off their wagons at the crest of the heights and slide them down the ravine to the river like a sled in snow. The uncontrollable pontoons made far too much noise in their dangerous descent and the idea soon abandoned.

As at the south end of town, work commenced on the bridges under the cover of darkness and fog. Their hulks steadily stretched out across the cold waters of the Rappahannock while Confederates on the far bank stayed their hand until the signal guns boomed at 5:00 a.m.

"I was standing at the extreme outer end of the bridge encouraging my men, when happening to cast my eyes to the shore beyond just as the fog lifted a little, I saw what for the moment almost chilled my blood," New York engineer Wesley Brainerd later wrote. "A long line of arms moving rapidly up and down was all I saw, for a moment later they were again obscured by the fog. But I knew too well that line of arms was ramming cartridges and that the crisis was near."

The 17th Mississippi and the 8th Florida—one of only three Florida regiments to serve in Lee's army at Fredericksburg—opened fire. "The bullets of the enemy rained upon my bridge," Brainerd said. "They went whizzing and zipping by and around me, pattering on the bridge, splashing into the water and thugging through the boats."

The same farcical tragedy between sharpshooters and

A monument to the 7th Michigan sits along Sophia Street at the upper crossing site.

Sketch of the river crossing.

The engineers made easy targets on the bridges.

engineers that unfolded at the Middle Crossing occurred here, too: engineers scurried to safety under fire, Federal infantry responded until Confederate fire stopped, the engineers returned to work, the Confederates returned to sharpshooting, over and over. "I was greatly mortified…to find that the pontoniers under my command would not continue to work until actually shot down," said their commander, Daniel Woodbury, released from arrest. "[T]he majority seemed to think their task a hopeless one. Perhaps I was unreasonable."

The subsequent artillery bombardment had as little effect at the Upper Crossing site as it had farther south. One observer considered it a lot of sound and fury signifying nothing. "The still air of the morning & the high, semicircle of frozen hills give rise to a tremendous echo which is so prolonged that there is hardly any cessation of sound & the battle seems more furious than it really is," he noted.

The heavy air of the cold morning made for a particularly surreal environment, a Confederate suggested. "Over and in the town the white winkings of the bursting shells reminded one of a countless swarm of fire-flies. Several buildings were set on fire, and their black smoke rose in remarkably slender,

A post-battle view of the upper crossing site.

straight, and tall columns for two hundred feet, perhaps, before they began to spread horizontally and unite in a great black canopy," he said.

When Hunt asked for infantry volunteers to cross the river, Colonel Norman Hall volunteered his battle-hardened 7th Michigan to force the crossing. The Michiganders piled into the boats, thirty-five to forty men each, six boats in all—but as the Michiganers jumped in, many of the engineers, who were supposed to ferry them across the river, jumped out. They'd been under fire most of the day and had endured enough. Some of the infantry wrestled the engineers back into their boats while others launched on their own. The Michiganders used their rifle butts to paddle. Some of their boats spun in circles, though, as one side paddled faster than the other. Some boats slowed due to mounting casualties. Southern marksmen kept up a murderous fire, undaunted by the Union artillery, which couldn't depress the barrels of their cannons low enough to keep the Confederates pinned down. William McCarter of 116th Pennsylvania later described the scene:

The steep slope leading to the crest of the riverbank offered protection to the Federals as they got closer to the Confederate side of the river. It shielded them from Confederates stationed in the houses along the far side of the road.

> *Hundreds of my comrades and I on the hilltops looked down on the brave fellows on the river, tugging and fighting with death itself. An oarsman would be seen relinquishing his oar and falling down dead or wounded in the bottom of his boat or overboard into the river. Then another would drop while not a few of their partners with rifles in hand were suffering a similar fate by their side. I think this was sad. It may have been the saddest sight during my life in the army.*

The topography itself finally provided relief. Confederates posted on the far side of Sophia Street couldn't fire down over the riverbank, which acted as a shield to protect the final stretch of the Union crossing. Soon, the flat noses of the boats hit dry land, and the Union soldiers spilled out onto the riverbank. Major Thomas Hunt, now in command of the Michiganders

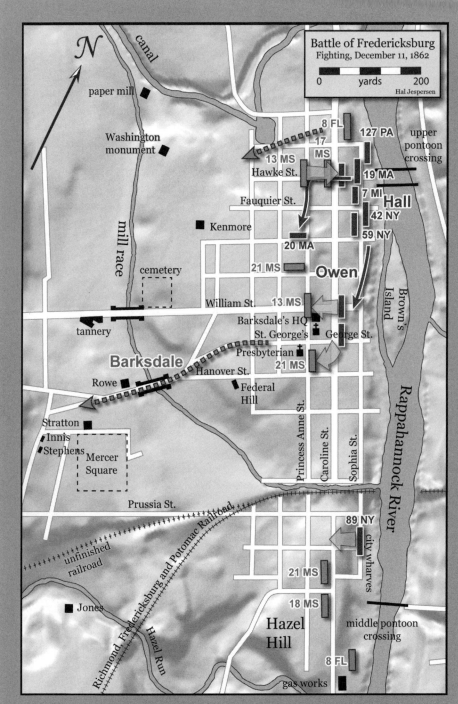

FIGHTING IN THE STREETS OF FREDERICKSBURG—Union and Confederate soldiers struggled for control of the city throughout December 11. Union soldiers crossed the Rappahannock River in pontoon boats and landed at the foot of Hawke Street and at the city docks. Eventually, Federals out-numbered and out-gunned the Southern riflemen, who, under the cover of darkness, retreated back to the main Confederate line, leaving the city in Union hands.

because the regiment's lieutenant colonel had been shot in the chest, gave the black-flag order to take no prisoners.

The Michiganders surged up the embankment across from the intersection of Hawke and Sophia streets, charging into the two houses that flanked the intersection. Observers from the Stafford side of the river could follow the fighting room by room, muzzle flash by muzzle flash.

More Federals rowed into the breach, including the 19th Massachusettes and the 20th Massachusetts, "The Harvard Regiment." Soon thereafter, the bedraggled engineers finished their work on the bridges, allowing more regiments to cross.

The flood of Union reinforcements presented a problem, though: there wasn't enough room on the far riverbank for all of them. The 7th Michigan had advanced only half a block before stopping in an alley, pinned down by Confederates who held the high ground. "Nearly every house and cellar had someone in it, firing from the windows," claimed one Union officer. Division commander Brigadier General Oliver Otis Howard ordered his men "to push ahead." No one wanted to take the lead under the galling Confederate fire.

The Harvard Regiment, disgusted with the Michiganders, steeled themselves and advanced. They pushed the rest of the way up Hawke Street and into the intersection with Caroline Street—where all of hell and damnation rained on them. Confederates fired from houses on all four sides of the intersection. The Federals deployed in the open streets as best they could: one company swung north into battle line on Caroline Street; another to the south; the third drove straight across the intersection and kept going alone into the heart of the city.

Although the Federal artillery barrage reduced much of the town to smoldering ruins, Federal infantry still met a hot reception when they stormed the city.

The 19th Massachusetts helped hold the bridgehead.

37

The Michiganders first advanced up Hawke Street, then took cover in an alleyway as Confederate fire against them picked up.

At the intersection of Hawke and Caroline streets, Confederates poured in fire from houses on all four corners.

"Here we cleared the houses near us, but shot came from far and near—we could see no one and were simply murdered," Captain George Macy of the 20th Massachusetts remembered. "[E]very shot of the enemy took effect. How I escaped I cannot say, as…more than a dozen [men] actually fell on me." In less than 20 minutes, one-third of the regiment were casualties.

Though less exposed, Confederates took their share of casualties, as well. Thin wood walls disintegrated under showers of bullets. Splinters hit Confederates in the eyes.

House by house, street by street, block by block, the fighting raged. By 4:30, there was little more Barksdale could do. The Federals outnumbered him nearly 3 to 1, and more were poised to cross. Finally, Barksdale's commander, Lafayette McLaws, reined in his pit-bull. As darkness fell, Barksdale ordered his men out of the city.

"Here at our feet lies the once beautiful city of Fredericksburg…" said a victorious Federal, who noted the "black pall of smoke from which at time could be seen… tongues of fire, darting upward from the exploding shells & from burning houses. Beyond the doomed city, on the opposite hills could be seen the frowning battlements of the enemy & in rear their numerous camps."

As the Federal army poured across the river, Lee was waiting.

At The Upper Crossing

A great number of firsts took place here on the banks of the Rappahannock: the first intentional artillery bombardment of an American city; the first riverine crossing under fire; the first major urban combat in the Civil War. Ambrose Burnside literally had to rewrite the rules of warfare as the battle unfolded—something he is usually given little credit for.

Standing at the foot of Hawke Street offers an excellent view of the riverbank and a glimpse of Chatham, atop the crest of Marye's Heights on the far side, through the trees. The steep slope of the riverbank offered protection to the Union troops as they tried to cross. The wooden pontoon boats that ferried were not built for speed, although they offered the advantage of flat noses that could be driven right up onto shore, allowing the infantry to leap out and stay relatively. The pontoon boats could be considered forerunners of the famed Higgins boats of World War II.

The Rappahannock River as seen from the upper crossing.

Two monuments mark the site of the Upper Pontoon Crossing. The first is a monument dedicated in December 1917 by the United Daughter of the Confederacy. The second is a five-ton, $10,000 monument, dedicated on August 31, 2003 that commemorates the actions of the Wolverines that came ashore.

Soldiers would have run up the riverbank past you and into many of the homes along Sophia Street, occupied then by Confederate infantry interspersed in the basements and throughout the first and second floors. Despite heavy small-arms and artillery fire, some of those original homes survived and still stand, although very few show any signs of war today.

As you walk up Hawke Street, you will notice a small alley on the left-hand side. This was the blind alley used to shield the 7th Michigan from Confederate fire spraying down the street from its intersection with Caroline Street ahead.

→ TO STOP 4

Return to your car. Follow Fauquier Street 0.1 miles to Princess Anne Street (Route 1/Route 17). *Please be cautious crossing over Caroline Street as you go.* Turn left onto Princess Anne Street. Princess Anne Street is a two-lane, one-way street. Follow Princess Anne Street 0.2 miles. Just past the second traffic light, park your car on either side of the street.

GPS Coordinates: N 38.30305 W 77.46035

A monument at the upper crossing site, installed in 1917, incorrectly cites Dec. 12, 1862 as the date of the crossing. A matching marker installed at the middle crossing site vanished into the river sometime around 1923.

The Occupation

CHAPTER FIVE

For an entire day, soldiers in the Army of the Potomac watched Confederate sharpshooters pick off their engineers and stymie their fellow infantrymen. As the death toll mounted and the advance delayed, their anger and frustration grew—dark, simmering emotions that stemmed back to the failure of the Peninsula Campaign and then rolled through Second Manassas, Antietam, and the loss of their beloved George McClellan.

By the time those soldiers did cross, their frustration had boiled over into wrath.

Burnside occupied the city with troops from the Second and Ninth corps, pushing skirmishers and scouts out to the city's far edge. Downtown, soldiers fanned out into the buildings and businesses of the city. "Here we stacked arms and the men were dismissed," recounted Lieutenant Josiah Favill of the 57th New York, who crossed with his division shortly after midnight:

> They immediately made a dash for the houses, and ransacked them from cellar to garret. Very soon the streets were filled with a motley crowd of men, some of them dressed in women's clothes, others with tall silk hats, curiously conspicuous…; many brought out sofas, chairs, etc., which were planted in the middle of the street, and the men proceeded to take their ease. Some carried pictures; one man had a fine stuffed alligator, and most of them had something. It was curious to observe these men upon the eve of a tremendous battle rid themselves of all anxiety by plunging into this boisterous sport. No attempt was made by the officers to interfere, and thus their minds were distracted….

The Presbyterian Church has a cannonball embedded in one of its front pillars. However, the cannonball isn't a leftover scar from the battle; it was placed there afterward as a prop.

"It was a very unpleasant sight to see the destruction of property; vandalism reigned supreme," another Federal wrote. "Men who at home were modest and unassuming now seemed to be possessed with an insatiate desire to destroy everything in sight."

The downtown was a wild scene of pandemonium. Fires still burned from the bombardment the day before while other fires were set by men in the street. Many attempted to get stolen

The Federal occupation of Fredericksburg represents one of the darkest days in American history.

goods back across the river and into the Union camps on Stafford Heights. "In a parlor of a very elegant house, only about half blown up on Caroline Street, I saw one soldier holding a cow by the horns and milking her into his canteen," one Federal soldier recalled.

In the midst of the chaos, civilians still lingered. Most had left the city before and during the bombardment, but perhaps as many as 1,000 civilians remained. Mamie Wells wrote of her experience dealing with the Union mob:

> *...that night! The pounding at our doors; the peering in the cellar windows by eyes red with intoxication; the oaths and curses; the ringing of axes and hammers; breaking in the tenantless houses; the firing of the buildings opposite; the insults heaped upon the occupants; the streets literally packed with soldiers in a complete state of moral demoralization...*

General Oliver Otis Howard took up residence in this private home along Princess Anne Street. The general forbade any plundering, although a resourceful private made off with a pie left on a window ledge to cool; the general never saw his dessert again.

Witnesses saw an old man rocking in a chair on a porch, laughing and talking to himself. Once a stately home, only the pillars and the porch remained; the rest had been reduced to a pile of smoking rubble.

Some homes, taken up as headquarters by general officers, were spared the enlisted men's wrath. One Federal "was ordered to take charge of a very fine house that Gen. Sully had selected as his headquarters. It was an elegant mansion and finely furnished," with a large and well-stocked library and an elegant piano. The walls of the rooms were hung with beautiful paintings and engravings and especially costly mirrors. "In the storeroom was a goodly supply of sugar, meat, flour, etc...."

The house, it turned out, belonged to Sully's brother-in-law, "a blamed rebel." Many of the home's paintings had actually been painted by the general's father, including a painting of the general himself, painted by his father when Sully was 3 or 4 years old. "The boys took nothing, and kept off all other marauders," a private said.

When Provost Marshall Marsena Patrick finally entered the city, he began arresting soldiers almost immediately. After hours of ransacking and stealing, the Federal mob was brought under control. "The sacking our soldiers gave the city was shameful," a Union doctor said. "The town was fairly turned inside out."

Others had little remorse. A soldier in the 140th New York wrote:

> *At the present time we are witnessing a splendid sight, as the city of Fredericksburg is on fire.... I call it beautiful because it is just the way that I wish to see our General's operate, for then I begin to think that they mean business... About half-past six all firing ceased, and your correspondent, with a number of others, enjoyed themselves witnessing the fiery flames as they spread through the doomed city of Fredericksburg. The sight was splendid....*

*   *   *

Despite the fact that he'd had nearly a month in which to prepare for his attack, Burnside felt he needed one more day. Rather than execute his plan, he spent the day consolidating his gains and finalizing details. "[H]e had no fixed plan of battle," grumbled Darius Couch. "After getting in the face of the enemy, his intentions seemed to be continually changing." Aside from some minor skirmishing and a lethargic artillery duel, the day frittered away.

At least it was so for the Federals. On the Confederate side, things were a far different matter. Weeks earlier, Lee had responded to Burnside's movement by sending Longstreet's

Hardly a building in Fredericksbur remained unscathed after the bombarment, street fighting, and occupation.

A diorama in the Battlefield Visitor Center (modeled after the photo top-left) recreated the devastation in the city's "Sandy Bottom" district.

The view from the Confederate artillery position atop Marye's Heights.

Col. E. Porter Alexander

First Corps into Fredericksburg to block any Union movement; his Second Corps, under Lieutenant General Thomas Jonathan "Stonewall" Jackson, had been deployed over a twenty-five mile line to the south to cover any movement Burnside might make in the direction of Port Royal. It wasn't until Burnside tipped his hand on December 11 that Lee knew for certain where the attack would come. He immediately sent word to Jackson to move all his troops toward Fredericksburg and link up on Longstreet's right.

Barksdale bought the Confederates a full day—more than Lee ever would have hoped for. Now Burnside gave Lee a second full day. It was all the time the gray fox needed to consolidate his own position, particularly on the south end of the field where Jackson's men would be stacked in depth to compensate for the terrain, which lacked the natural strength of the northern end of Lee's line. There, Howison Hill, Telegraph Hill, and the series of hills collectively known as Marye's Heights gave Confederates a significant topographical advantage.

Even there, Confederates weren't content to sit and wait. Colonel E. Porter Alexander, head of the First Corps' artillery, fortified his positions along the top of the heights. As he and Longstreet looked over the open fields that ran down toward town, Alexander said matter-of-factly, "we can cover that ground…so well that we comb it as with a fine-tooth comb. A chicken could not live on that field when we open on it." He was not bragging.

Burnside half-hoped Lee would withdraw in the face of such a formidable host, but Lee understood the strength of his position, made even stronger by Burnside's delay. Battle, Lee knew, would come soon enough.

In Downtown Fredericksburg

You are standing in the heart of downtown Fredericksburg. The city sits on a plateau and from here, at its highest point, you can look back along Princess Anne Street toward the William Street intersection and see how the ground slopes downward.

Old Slave Block, used before the Civil War for the Sale and Annual Hire of Slaves

A slave auction block at the intersection of William and Charles streets, once featured in a series of postcards that highlighted Fredericksburg's historical attractions, still serves as a haunting reminder.

The city boasted three major churches, two of which are at the southern end of this block: St. George's Episcopal Church and the Presbyterian Church, which has a postwar cannonball embedded as a prop in one of the large front pillars. Along the outer brick wall of the church, at the corner of the Princess Anne Street and George Street, you will see a plaque that claims "GEN. STONEWALL JACKSON, BY GEN. LEE'S REQUEST, ON THIS CORNER, PLANNED THE BATTLE OF FREDERICKSBURG." Longstreet, not Jackson, had been charged with the city's defense even while Jackson was still in the Shenandoah Valley and, later, southeast of the city near Port Royal.

Today, downtown Fredericksburg hosts several great attractions, including the Fredericksburg Area Museum, which tells the story of the city from its Pre-Revolutionary Era founding to the modern day. The Fredericksburg City Visitor Center on Caroline Street offers information on all museums, attractions, and restaurants.

For more information on the history of the city, see Appendix A.

Dedicated by the United Daughters of the Confederacy in November 1924 at a cost of $25, a plaque outside the Presbyterian Church ascribes a mythical but patently false role to Stonewall Jackson, who probably never even set foot in the city prior to the battle.

➤ TO STOP 5

Follow Princess Anne Street to Lafayette Boulevard 0.4 miles. At the traffic light, turn right. At the next traffic light, turn left onto Charles Street (Route 17). Follow Charles Street 0.2 miles and bear right onto Dixon Street. Follow Dixon Street 2.3 miles—Dixon Street will turn into Tidewater Trail—and turn right into the Slaughter Pen Farm. The farm will be marked with signs by the Civil War Trust.

GPS Coordinates: N 38° 26448 W 77° 26.44125

The old Market House served as the economic and cultural center of town. During the battle on December 11, William Barksdale set up his headquarters here. Today, it houses the Fredericksburg Area Museum.

The Slaughter Pen

CHAPTER SIX

The morning of December 13, 1862, dawned foggy and cold across the Rappahannock River Valley. More ominously for Union Major General William B. Franklin, the morning dawned under the fog of war.

A little over a mile south of the city, where Federal engineers had constructed the lowermost pontoon bridge on December 11 virtually unopposed, Franklin's Left Grand Division awaited orders that had not yet arrived.

The previous evening at a Council of War, Burnside had finalized a battle plan that consisted of a two-pronged simultaneous assault on the Confederate line. The assaults, aimed at both Prospect Hill and Marye's Heights, were to begin before dawn. Burnside confirmed the plan with his subordinates and, satisfied that everyone understood, sent everyone away with a promise to follow up with written orders.

But Franklin's orders didn't arrive before the planned jump-off time. The courier, Brigadier General James Hardie of Burnside's staff, had been severely hampered by icy roads and so did not arrive until 7:30 a.m. When Franklin read the delayed communiqué, his frustration deepened. As he had correctly understood it the night before, his assault against Prospect Hill was to be the main attack, but Burnside's written orders no longer seemed to reflect that:

> *keep your whole command in position for a rapid movement down the Old Richmond Road and…send…a division at least…to seize, if possible, the height near Captain Hamilton's…taking care to keep it well supported and its line of retreat open.*

From the Slaughter Pen Farm looking toward Prospect Hill.

"A great captain would have cast [the orders] aside and assumed responsibility," one of Franklin's subordinates later wrote. However, already well behind schedule as he was, Franklin decided not to ask Burnside for clarification, nor did he ask for

The Bowling Green Road.

clarification from the sheepish Hardie, who failed to offer any. Thus, Franklin misinterpreted his role entirely and assumed his assault would support a main assault against Marye's Heights. Instead of sending his 65,000 infantrymen against Prospect Hill, he called on only a single division—4,500 men—from John Reynolds' First Corps. Franklin instructed Reynolds to keep the division well supported.

Reynolds chose the men of Major General George G. Meade's Pennsylvania Reserves Division, a battle-hardened group of men Reynolds himself had once commanded. Meade, known by many as a "google-eyed snapping turtle," had graduated from West Point and served in the pre-war army as an engineer. Wounded at the Battle of Glendale, Meade returned to fight at Second Manassas, South Mountain, and Antietam. By the time of Fredericksburg, he was the junior-most major general in the Army of the Potomac.

As the spearhead of the assault, Meade's division deployed a quarter mile south of a property known today as the Slaughter Pen Farm. In support on Meade's left, Brigadier General Abner Doubleday deployed his division—although Doubleday's men would soon veer off, completely sidetracked, to deal with a single Confederate cannon commanded by a young Confederate artillerist, Major John Pelham. Doubleday would be useless to Meade.

To Meade's right deployed the division of Brigadier General John Gibbon. Gibbon had three full brigades—just over 4,000 men—arrayed in three lines of battle. Brigadier General Nelson Taylor led the first; Colonel Peter Lyle led the second; Colonel Adrian Root led the third. Gibbon, a North Carolinian who chose to stay with the Union, didn't know it

Maj. Gen. William B. Franklin

At the Slaughter Pen Farm:
modern views of the attack
field Maj. Gen. George Meade
sent his men across (top)
toward Prospect Hill
(the rise in the treeline
at the center of the picture)
and the attack field
Brig. Gen. John Gibbon
sent his men across
(toward the lone tree
at the end of the treeline).

yet, but he would end up assaulting a Confederate brigade that
included three of his brothers.

Franklin started things off at 11:00 a.m.—some six hours
late—with an artillery barrage from eleven batteries. Sixty-six
guns blasted away for an hour. "[T]he air was resonant with
the savage music of shells and solid shot," one Federal wrote.
The Confederates, meanwhile, remained silent.

At noon, Meade sent his men forward. Confederates let
them get within 800 yards of their line before they finally
opened with a withering barrage of their own. Artillery
massed on Prospect Hill, around Bernard's Cabins, and near
Hamilton's Crossing poured onto Meade's and Gibbon's
men, who dove for cover in the muddy fields. The Federal
bombardment, it turned out, had done little to soften the
Confederate position because the far woodline had obscured
the targets. Once their Southern counterparts opened fire,
though, they revealed themselves to the Federals, whose
accuracy improved significantly. The infantry could do little
but wait for the artillerists to settle the matter between them.

Maj. Gen. John Reynolds

Maj. Gen. George Gordon Meade (left)

Brig. Gen. John Gibbon (right)

"[T]he cannon balls were flying over and among us all the time, killing men and hosses and tearing up the ground all around us and throwing the mud and dirt all over us and blew up one of our ammunition wagons," a Pennsylvanian said.

During the barrage, Meade did his best to keep his men calm. When he rode up to Colonel William "Buck" McCandless, Meade had an uncharacteristic smile on his face. "A star this morning, William?" Meade asked, referring to a possible promotion for the colonel. "More likely a wooden overcoat," McCandless responded. Within seconds, a shell arched in and gutted Buck's horse. After the initial shock, the two officers tried to laugh off the incident as McCandless pulled himself from the mud.

Around 12:45 p.m., Federal gunners struck two limber chests full of ammunition, which went up with a spectacular pyrotechnics show that drew the men of Meade's division to their feet with a cheer. The crusty Meade realized it was "go" time, and he drove his three brigades toward a point of woods across the field.

Meade's sudden burst of speed and daring caught Gibbon off guard. Left literally lying on their bellies, his men got to their feet and Gibbon got them into alignment. This was his first action as a division commander, and he wanted to make sure he got the details right, but in doing so, precious minutes ticked away.

Taylor's brigade, caked with mud and soaking wet, led the way across the muddy fields. Soon, they came upon a ditch fence nearly four feet deep and partially filled with cold water. After traversing that and getting back into formation, they crested a small rise and discovered more than half the field still stretched out ahead of them. Onward they went, down a gently rolling slope toward the Richmond, Fredericksburg and Potomac Rail Road.

During the battle, ditch fences were nearly impossible to make out in the distance, and many front-line soldiers marched squarely and unknowingly into them.

The boys in blue made it to within 150 yards of the rail line before Confederate infantry unleashed its first volleys on them. Confederate Brigadier General James Lane had five North Carolina regiments on line compared to Taylor's four. Artillery support from Lane's left at Bernard's Cabins added to the Yankee woes. "It seemed that the front column melted away," a North Carolinian recalled.

In fact, two of Taylor's regiments did break and run for the rear, but help was on the way from Lyle's men, who were advancing to take up the fight. Lyle's six regiments added their weight to Taylor's remaining two, and all six advanced toward the rail line, drawing within forty-five yards before bogging down in a slugfest. Both sides quickly ran low on ammunition, and Federal commanders fell thick and fast. Mere captains were left in charge of entire regiments, a prelude to the war to come in 1864.

With his division again stopped, Gibbon's final brigade approached the front. Adrian Root, a civilian turned soldier, pressed the attack with his five regiments. Joined by Gibbon himself, they smashed the Confederate defensive line.

As Gibbon's men poured into the woods, James Lane and his unlucky North Carolinians needed help fast. It came from Brigadier General Edward Thomas' four Georgia regiments and Brigadier General Dorsey Pender's four North Carolina regiments. With eight fresh Rebel regiments pushing back at them, the disorganized Union division crumbled under the pressure, pulling back first to the rail line, then back across the field to the Bowling Green Road and the safety of the Federal gun line. During the melee, Gibbon was wounded in the wrist by an artillery fragment.

Confederates did try to mount a pursuit, but as they appeared on the western edge of the open fields, concentrated

Brig. Gen. James Lane

Brig. Gen. David Birney

artillery fire quickly discouraged them. Their momentum still carried them forward enough to engage the few reinforcements sent to aide Gibbon and Meade, who had scored a far more dramatic breakthrough to the south, only to be repulsed as well.

Brigadier General David Birney's Third Corps division had marched his 7,000 men across the bridges at the Lower Crossing and, making his way to the front, positioned himself to stop any Confederate counterattacks. One of his brigades, that of Brigadier General J. H. Hobart Ward, advanced as far as the southwest corner of the Slaughter Pen Farm, where they ran into the Confederate pursuit. Colonel Edmund Atkinson's brigade of Georgians hit Ward in the flank, but they, in turn, met grief from another of Birney's brigades. "[O]ur men had to choose between a surrender or retreat under fire…or flee for their lives back to the protection of the woods," one of the Georgians said. With Federal artillery also raining upon them, Confederates chose the latter option and withdrew back into the safety of the woods even as the Federals withdrew to the safety of the Bowling Green Road.

By 3:00 p.m., the major action on the south end of the battlefield had ended. Ambrose Burnside had just lost his best chance at winning the battle of Fredericksburg. No one realized how close a thing it had been though—no one, that is, except for George Gordon Meade, the ol' snapping turtle himself.

Meade had snapped Stonewall Jackson's line in two.

At Slaughter Pen Farm

This 216-acre farm is preserved for future generations thanks to the combined efforts of the Civil War Trust, the Central Virginia Battlefields Trust, and the National Park Service. In 2006, the CWT purchased the land for $12 million, saving it from industrial development. Although sprawl has crept into the Fredericksburg area, this piece of land remains an historical oasis, preserving the last open attack plain on the Fredericksburg Battlefield.

The parking area sits about 100 yards behind the Federal artillery line. Massed in the fields to your right and behind you were the men of Brigadier General John Gibbon's First Corps division. Gibbon's assault, made with a compact front, would have swept over the ground between the modern barns, which were not on the field at the time of the battle, and the Shannon Airport to the north. Major General George Gordon Meade massed his men behind you and to the left toward an area occupied by a modern industrial complex.

One Third Corps unit, the 114th Pennsylvania Infantry, known as Collis's Zouaves, marched into action here for the

first time. A painting by Carl Rochling, which hangs in the Fredericksburg Battlefield Visitor Center, depicts their assault.

During the melee in the field to your front, a counterattack by Confederate Colonel Edmund Atkinson went afoul, and Federals took Atkinson prisoner—the only brigade commander captured at the battle of Fredericksburg. His aide, Captain James Van Vulkenburg, was captured, too, by a soldier in the 7th Pennsylvania Reserves. Van Vulkenburg was eventually paroled, but he came back to haunt the Pennsylvanians. On May 5, 1864, at the Battle of the Wilderness, Van Vulkenburg and a handful of men who were cut off from the rest of their unit came upon some Federals in the dark, close wood. Van Vulkenburg bluffed about the number of men with him, enabling him to capture the entire 7th Pennsylvania Reserves, thus returning the favor.

If you choose to follow the trail laid out by the Civil War Trust, please stay on the marked path, and please refrain from entering the farm buildings, which are not open to the public. A dozen interpretive markers explain the battle and help to orient you with excellent maps.

The fields of the Slaughter Pen Farm look much like they did in 1862. On the morning of December 13, though, the fields were churned up by thousands of men and horses. Snow and rain from earlier weeks made the fields, at places, like a quagmire.

If you follow the path about fifty feet beyond the silo,

After preserving the Slaughter Pen Farm, the Civil War Trust established a walking trail. The field's topography is deceptive, and a walk along the trail offers visitors a chance to see how the terrain unfolds and perspectives change.

On the far side of the Slaughter Pen Farm, looking back toward the Bowling Green Road, which is totally obscured by the deceptive terrain.

you'll notice that the land between this point and Route 2/ Route 17 (the road that brought you here) is relatively flat. Looking north of the trail (to the right), you'll notice the field ever-so-gently rises to form a slight ridge. Already, as a trip across the field will demonstrate, the topography begins to play tricks.

Another sixty-five yards brings you up suddenly on a Virginia ditch fence. Front-line soldiers stumbled into them unexpectedly. Because of the winter weather, the fences were filled with three to four feet of ice cold water. Soaked, muddied, and cold, the soldiers had no choice but to press on.

Follow the trail another thirty yards and turn right, following the trail north for another fifty yards. The building by the elbow in the path was not there at the time of the battle, but a small cabin did once stand in this vicinity, along with a shed, a blacksmith shop, and a tobacco barn. This was the home of Robert Brooks, the overseer of the Mannsfield slaves. On many post-battle maps, his cabin appears as the Burnt Chimneys. On the evening of December 12th, a detachment of Dorsey Pender's North Carolina brigade sneaked into the field and put the torch to the home, fearing that Federal sharpshooters would occupy the structure. Chips and chunks of red brick—remains from the Brooks homestead—still turn up in this area.

This small ridgeline bisects the attack plain roughly north-south. Approaching the ridge, the treeline doesn't appear too far away; reaching the ridge reveals just how much more field remains to cross. It also offered Union infantrymen their first full view of the Confederate position. Most of the morning, the men had been massed facedown in the open fields, so the panorama revealed to them when they reached this spot might've felt a little sickening, especially once Confederate artillery opened on them from Bernard's Cabins, the open knoll to your front right.

As you continue down the trail, just before it turns left, you'll see the hangers on the edge of Shannon Airport. From that area, a Pennsylvania Battery fired on the Confederate position along the tree and rail line. This area also marks the extreme right flank of Gibbon's assault column. From where you are standing, it would be impossible to see to the left flank because of undulations in the topography. You may notice, as you walk, that some places offer views of the whole field while others offer sightlines of little more than twenty yards to the left or right. Taylor's brigade, leading the advance, took higher losses as they stepped closer toward the Confederate line, but because of the topography, his left wing initially didn't take as many as his right. As the topography continued to roll, that quickly changed.

The Federal line moved forward toward the large, lone tree on this side of the rail line. The small knoll where the tree sits blocked the view of Lane's two centermost regiments, but as Federals got closer, the tree provided little cover. The Union advance stalled near the rail line, drove across, and was then finally repulsed.

A member of the 114th Pennsylvania Infantry— Collis's Zouaves. The French-style uniforms featured red caps and pantaloons, gold sashes, and ornately embroidered blue jackets.

In and around this field, no fewer than six Medals of Honor were awarded to Union soldiers for their heroism during the December 13 battle: John Shiel of the 90th Pennsylvania disobeyed orders and risked his life to retrieve wounded comrades; Martin Shubert and Joseph Kenne of the 26th New York Infantry bore their regimental flag during the battle and brought it off the field safely; Colonel Charles Collis of the 114th Pennsylvania grasped the colors of his regiment and shouted "Remember Kernstown!" while leading a counterattack; George E. Maynard of the 13th Massachusetts reentered the field to retrieve a fallen comrade when his unit had withdrawn; Philip Petty took up the discarded colors of the green 136th Pennsylvania, helping to steady the wavering regiment.

⟶ TO STOP 6

Turn right onto Route 2/Route 17 and follow the road for 1.2 miles. At the traffic light at Benchmark Road, turn right. Follow Benchmark Road (Route 608) 0.1 miles and turn left into the parking lot of the 7-11 complex and park. The monument and markers are near the intersection of Tidewater Trail and Benchmark Road.

GPS Coordinates: N 38.25220 W 77.42623

The Gallant Pelham

CHAPTER SEVEN

He was young, handsome, talented, charismatic and courageous—and impatient enough to go looking for trouble as he watched John Reynolds' First Corps assembling in the distance. John Pelham, first lieutenant of artillery, twenty-two years old, gathered up his gun crew and a single 12-pounder Napoleon and set out to meet the enemy.

Born near Alexandria, Alabama, on September 7, 1838, Pelham was a natural and gifted horseman. In 1856, he accepted an appointment to West Point, but by 1861, with war looming, the young cadet withdrew from the academy a week shy of his graduation. (His class, the "war class" of 1861, was the only five-year class in the history of the academy).

Pelham followed a circuitous route south to cross the Mason-Dixon line—from New York to New Albany, Indiana, then across the Ohio into Kentucky—to offer his services to the Confederacy. When word spread of his intentions, Union officials placed him under surveillance and tried to prevent him from crossing, but Pelham eluded them.

He was commissioned a first lieutenant of artillery and stationed in Winchester, Virginia. Shortly thereafter, during the Battle of First Manassas, he caught the eye of Colonel James Ewell Brown Stuart, who authorized the brash lieutenant to put together a six-piece battery of horse artillery. It became known as Stuart's horse artillery, and Pelham commanded it with daring and skill. His men fought well at Second Manassas, Antietam, and other engagements in between.

Now, at Fredericksburg, Pelham looked to make his mark again. With the Federal First Corps advancing from the river toward Prospect Hill, Pelham planned to trip them up. From the Confederate line, he and his men advanced along the Mine Road to the intersection of the Bowling Green Road, and there, he found a perfect feature in the terrain for his gun: a slight depression on the southwest corner, obscured by a line of cedar trees growing along the road.

The Pelham monument was placed at the intersection in 1903 by former Stonewall Jackson staff officer James Power Smith—one of ten markers Smith placed on and around the Fredericksburg-area battlefields.

While at West Point, comrades gave John Pelham the nickname "Sallie" because of his boyish features.

Pelham rolled his single cannon into the depression and his men readied it for action. They then rolled it up just far enough for the muzzle to peek out from the cedars. They sighted the gun, then fired—the recoil of the gun rolling it back into the depression, hidden, where it could be reloaded for the next shot.

From his concealed position, Pelham fired into the left flank of Reynolds' assault columns, enfilading the line. Pelham's cannonballs could also roll up the left flank of Major General George Gordon Meade's division, as well as Brigadier General John Gibbon's division, who all threw themselves prostate in the open muddy fields. Reynolds' assault stumbled to a halt. Pelham's lone gun helped stop the initial Union assault against Prospect Hill.

"When thus standing in line a cannon boomed out on our left, at close range, seemingly on the Bowling Green road," said Bates Alexander of the 7th Pennsylvania Reserves. "[A] shot whizzed high in the air passing over our heads from left to right along the line. Naturally supposing, from the position, 'twas one of our own batteries, we thought our gunners had had too much 'commissary' this morning, and so remarked. Another report, then a third, each time the missile coming lower in the air, when they discovered 'twas the enemy. The order was given 'down.' when from the force of the custom we fell forward face downward…"

Pelham's gunners not only targeted infantry; they targeted Federal batteries as well, knocking out one of the guns of Battery B 1st Pennsylvania Light Artillery.

The Federals quickly tired of the pest firing in on their flank. Six Union batteries fired toward his position. Long guns from across the Rappahannock tried to join in, too, but found they could not depress their barrels far enough to strike the area. Complicating matters, a morning fog still hung low over the cedars and filled the depression, obscuring Pelham's exact position from any Federal gunners.

Finally, Federal infantry from Major General Abner Doubleday's division tried to root out the Confederates. Well-placed Confederate cavalry screened the front and protected Pelham, though his crew had to cease firing so they would not give away their exact position.

Stuart sent a message to the major, asking how everything was going. Pelham, sitting with one leg across the top of his saddle, responded, "I am doing first rate." And so it remained for nearly an hour. All went well for Pelham.

To bolster Pelham's firepower, Stuart dispatched another cannon, a Blakely rifled cannon. As it moved into position, Federals clearly saw it, and since there was not enough room in the depression for the Blakely, it provided an easy target. The gun suffered a direct hit from its Union counterparts.

Federal pressure and diminishing ammunition began to finally force Pelham from his position. As his gunner poured canister into the blue ranks, Pelham gave the order to limber up and pull out. They made their way safely back to Confederate lines.

Pelham would survive the battle, only to fall mortally wounded in a cavalry charge the following March. Fredericksburg proved to be his finest day. His ingenuity and skill proved more than a match for his counterparts, allowing him to stall the entire Federal advance on the south end of the field for nearly an hour. His efforts were praised by both Jeb Stuart and Robert E. Lee. Lee went as far to dub the young officer as "the gallant Pelham."

At Pelham's Crossing

In 1862, the area now known as Pelham's Crossing was fairly wide open, although cedar trees lined the roads and ditch fences cut across the land. To his left was Prospect Hill, just over one-half mile to the west; to his right were open fields leading one-quarter of a mile to the Rappahannock. Pelham's gun would have been positioned facing north, looking toward the modern self-storage facility. If not for the cedars, depression, and fog, Union gunners would have wreaked havoc on him within minutes. As it was, he and his men had a perfect angle on the left flank of Reynolds' assault column.

The area around the Pelham marker bustles with traffic, so visitors should exercise caution getting in and out of the parking area.

Standing near the intersection of Tidewater Trail and Benchmark Road today are two interpretive markers and a low stone monument. The marker once sat about ten feet closer to Route 2/Route 17, but when the Virginia Department of Transportation widened the road in 2006, the monument was uprooted. It spent many months lying on its side before being reset in its current location.

⟶ TO STOP 7

Turn left onto Benchmark Road (Route 608). Follow Benchmark Road 0.9 miles. Turn right onto Mine Run Road (Route 636) and follow it for 2.3 miles. At the intersection of Mine Run Road and Landsdowne Road, turn right onto Landsdowne Road (Route 638). Follow Lansdowne Road 0.9 miles and turn right onto Lee Drive. Follow Lee Drive 1.6 miles and park on the left at the Federal Breakthrough. *On the Park Service's driving tour, this is tour stop five, "Union Breakthrough."*

GPS Coordinates: N 38° 25149 W 77° 44391

The Breakthrough

CHAPTER EIGHT

Stonewall Jackson was glad to see the Yankees coming, he said. "[M]y men may sometimes fail to take a position," he told a staff officer, "but to defend one, never!"

With the blue horde amassing on the far side of the valley, some Confederates worried they'd be eaten up. Jackson had no such doubts. He had spent two days consolidating his position on the southern end of the Southern line, stacking and overlapping his divisions four deep: Major General A. P. Hill's men in front with the divisions of Major General Daniel Harvey Hill, Brigadier General Jubal Early, and Brigadier General William Taliaferro stacked behind. From the bottomlands along Lansdowne Run, where his segment of the line joined with Longstreet's First Corps, southward to Prospect Hill, Jackson had four men for every foot of ground he had to cover.

Midway along his line, A. P. Hill—called "Little Powell" by some—had left a 600-yard gap in the line where it crossed through a marsh. Hill contended that the boggy ground was impenetrable, and Jackson and Lee agreed. Brigade commanders James Lane and James Archer, who held ground on either side of the gap and would therefore have vulnerable flanks exposed to the gap, both protested, so Hill placed the brigade of Brigadier General Maxcy Gregg in reserve behind the marsh.

Gregg, a South Carolina native and strong proponent of states' rights, had five regiments from his home state under his command. In reserve as they were, the men had arms stacked. Some were enjoying late breakfasts while others relaxed and tried to keep warm around campfires.

Into the gap in the Confederate line, and into the unsuspecting camps of Gregg's brigade, stormed George Meade's Pennsylvania Reserves.

In their advance across the open killing fields south of the Slaughter Pen Farm, Meade's men had taken heavy casualties from the artillery posted on Prospect Hill as well as from Lane's

Beyond the interpretive markers at the breakthrough site, the ground drops off to the low, marshy area that served as an open door for Federals.

61

Lt. Gen. Thomas "Stonewall" Jackson once boasted that his "men may sometimes fail to take a position, but to defend one, never!" —a statement sorely tested at Fredericksburg.

and Archer's infantry. "It was terrible to see the men falling all about…" one of them recalled. "The balls humming and shizzing about us like bees and such a roar of cannon and muskets that one could hardly hear the orders of our officers."

Looking for any cover they could find, Colonel William Sinclair's brigade spotted a finger of woods jutting like an oasis into the field. Even more astoundingly, no Confederate rifle fire came from those woods. Sinclair's men veered there for protection even as the other lead brigade, under Brigadier General Conrad F. Jackson, pushed onward toward Prospect Hill. Jackson's men made their way nearly to the rail line before they halted and began firing at the heights. However, standing in the open field—"under a murderous fire that mowed them down like grass," said a unit chaplain—was not the best idea. They began falling by scores. Survivors dove for cover among the rail line and ditches at the base of the hill as Confederates poured volley after volley into them.

Sinclair's men in the woods found themselves skirting the swamp that Hill had deemed impassable by any organized body of men—but by now, unit cohesion among the Federals had broken down almost completely. They were anything but organized. Sinclair went down with an injured ankle. Another brigade commander, Colonel Albert Magilton, was trapped beneath his horse when it was killed. At the foot of Prospect Hill, a bullet to the face killed Conrad Jackson.

And so it was, more a mob than an army, that Meade's men clambered through the swamp and up the hilly terrain into Gregg's camps, driven more by adrenaline and momentum than leadership.

Gregg had posted a picket line along the rail line, in front of the swamp, in the event of an attack. So overwhelming had been Sinclair's push to the woods, though, that in order to avoid capture, the Confederate skirmishers fled southward down the railroad—not back to the rear to warn the rest of the brigade. Not until bullets began to clip tree branches and plug into tree trunks around them did Gregg's reserve brigade realize trouble was scrambling toward them.

Some of the Palmetto State men reached for their rifles. Officers started to get their men in a line of battle. Suddenly Gregg suddenly appeared. When he saw the men of Orr's Rifles readying for combat, he chastised them for taking up their rifles. It was their own men in their front, he told them, worried that the brigade would inflict friendly-fire casualties on Confederate units to their front.

Gregg was partially deaf, though, and could not fully hear the volume of fire coming from his front. Nor did he see the Pennsylvanians approach, distracted as he was by his own men. But someone saw him. On horseback, he made the perfect target, and a Federal marksman hit him. The bullet ripped into Gregg's side, severing his spine and reeling him from his saddle. His men eventually moved the paralyzed general to Thomas Yerby's home, Belvoir, where he died two days later.

The Pennsylvania Reserves swarmed through Orr's Rifles and into the 1st South Carolina, who soon fell into rout. "They were cooking coffee and eating dinner we captured all their guns that were stacked, also their colors on top of their guns," a member of the 30th Pennsylvania said. Next to fall were the 12th and 13th South Carolina. In less than twenty minutes, one of the finest brigades of the Army of Northern Virginia was swept wholesale from the field.

With the South Carolinians gone, Federals fanned out, north and south. The ol' snapping turtle had snapped the Confederate line in two, and now his men looked to bust it wide open.

Brig. Gen. Maxy Gregg

At The Federal Breakthrough

The road known today as Lee Drive dates back to 1722. As far back as pre-Revolution days, farmers and travelers—who knew it as Massaponax Road—used the road as a shortcut between other main roads in the area. At the time of the battle of Fredericksburg, the road was little more than an improved dirt path with heavy woods on either side, yet it served as the backbone of the communication, supply, and troop-movement system of Lee's army on Stonewall Jackson's front.

After the battle, in a statement to the Joint Committee on the Conduct of the War (right), Burnside claimed that Massaponax Road was one of his objectives during the fight. It can be surmised that Burnside intended to use the road as an axis of advance—meaning that once Confederates had been dislodged from Prospect Hill and the road, Burnside's men could advance northward, rolling up the Confederate right flank while making frontal assaults against its left. If all went well, Lee's men would be smashed against the Rappahannock River or at least be forced to give up their blocking position along the heights. It's worth noting, however, that Burnside never outlined any such thing in the attack orders he passed along to Franklin.

➔ TO STOP 8

Follow Lee Drive 0.5 miles to its terminus at Prospect Hill and park in the designated parking area. *On the Park Service's driving tour, this is tour stop six, "Prospect Hill."*

GPS Coordinates: 38° 24.810 W 77°.43588

The enemy had cut a road… in the rear of the line of heights…by means of which they connected the two wings of their army, and avoided a long detour around through bad country. I obtained from a colored man from the other side of the town information in regard to this new road, which proved to be correct. I wanted to obtain possession of that new road, and that was my reason for making an attack on the extreme [Union] left. I did not intend to make the attack on the [Union] right until that position had been taken, which I supposed would stagger the enemy, cutting their line in two; and then I proposed to make a direct attack on their front, and drive them out of their works.

— Ambrose Burnside

Prospect Hill

CHAPTER NINE

Ambrose Powell Hill might have had a touch of prescience in him—events played out to suggest it, at any rate.

His relationship with his corps commander, Stonewall Jackson, had never been good and, as November had dragged into December, the breach only worsened. The two men barely tolerated each other, despite the skill they each showed on the battlefield, and Jackson had once gone so far as to place Hill under arrest. Before hostilities broke out between Union and Confederate forces at Fredericksburg, hostilities had been on the verge of breaking out again between Hill and Jackson. Threats of court-martial circulated freely by both men.

"I suppose I am to vegetate here all the winter under that crazy old Presbyterian fool," Hill groused to Stuart. "I am like the porcupine all bristles, and all sticking out, too, so I know we shall have a smash up before long…. The almighty will get tired of helping Jackson after a while, and then he'll get the damndest thrashing…[though] I shall get my share and probably all the blame, for the people never blame Stonewall for any disaster."

Now that thrashing had come. Meade's Pennsylvania Reserves had smashed through the gap in Hill's line—a gap Jackson and Lee had both known about and consented to—and it looked all the world like "Little Powell" was going to take the fall for it.

As Meade's men fed into the gap, they fanned out. To the north, they collided with James Lane's brigade, which was also starting to feel pressure from Gibbon on its front. To the south, Meade's men drove toward James Archer's brigade, anchored on the flank by the 19th Georgia. Unfortunately, the Georgians themselves weren't anchored on anything more than a small knoll a few hundred feet outside of the woodline. Already contending with Colonel Jackson's brigade in front of them, the Georgians hardly expected Federals to approach from their flank and rear, especially when those mud-covered Federals looked like butternut-clad Confederates.

Maj. Gen. A. P. Hill

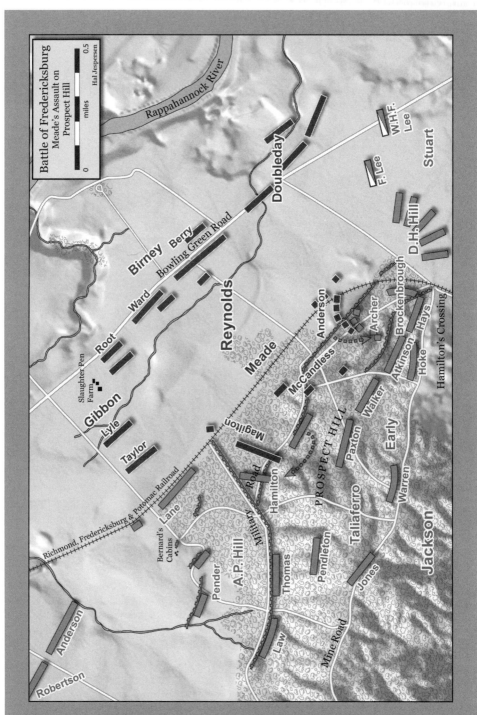

THE BATTLE FOR PROSPECT HILL—Prospect Hill was the most closely contested action on December 13. Union soldiers under George Meade and John Gibbon succeeded in breaking the Confederate line. Though Federal reinforcements were close at hand, most simply sat and watched the battle from the Bowling Green Road. Fast-moving Confederate counterattacks swept Meade and Gibbon back, shutting the door on Burnside's best chance at victory.

A monument erected by former Jackson staff officer James Power Smith still stands on Prospect Hill to mark Jackson's presence there during the battle.

That gave those Yankees all the time they needed to hit Archer's men squarely in the flank. The "damndest thrashing" continued.

*   *   *

The morning had thus far gone well for Jackson's men positioned on Prospect Hill. Atop the high ground, "Old Blue Light" had deployed fourteen guns under the capable command of Lieutenant Colonel Reuben L. Walker—supposedly the handsomest man in the Confederacy. Walker placed the bulk of his guns along the southern end of the hill and protected them with crescent-shaped earthworks called lunettes. Archer's mixed brigade of Georgia, Alabama, and Tennessee regiments supported Walker's guns. The infantrymen dug a line of rifle pits, and some tore up ties from the railroad to utilize in their defenses.

When the Federal artillery bombardment opened at 11:00 a.m., Jackson sat stoically on his horse, Little Sorrell, as shells came crashing in. He ordered his artillerists to withhold any

Brig. Gen. James Archer

67

Meade's men attack Prospect Hill.

return fire so as to not give away their position.

"What an awful suspense these last moments are," a Confederate artillerist recalled. "The gun is charged, lanyard in hand, the gunner at the trail, ammunition heaped in piles nearby, waiting for the order to fire. Minutes seem like hours. One holds his breath and then breathes hard. But at last the moment comes."

Jackson, himself an artillerist during the Mexican War and an artillery instructor at the Virginia Military Institute, waited until the initial Federal advance got within 800 yards before signaling his artillery to finally open fire. "A raise of the hand…and the fourteen guns…let loose at the same instant," the artillerist said. "From then on, it is load and fire, load and fire, as fast as sponge and rammer and lanyard can do their work, and as fast as muscle and skill and consuming zeal can direct and control."

The infantry went to ground while Federal artillery responded—and this time, with targets to shoot at, the Federal fire was much more deadly. James Archer, a slight, frail man who had only that morning returned from a field hospital to rejoin his men for battle, took to his horse to set a bold example. One of his staff officers took to horse as well but was quickly decapitated by a shell.

For Captain William Pegram's gunners, the strain became too much, and they bolted rearward. To shame them back into line, Pegram wrapped himself in a Confederate battle flag and stalked angrily between his guns until his men slunk back.

"It was a time to test a man's courage," one Confederate admitted.

Falling tree branches, clipped off by shells, also became a hazard. Incoming shells kicked up icy mud. It was pandemonium. Jackson remained stoic, and some witnesses even made the improbable claim that Little Sorrell slept through the entire cacophony.

The battle flag of the 19th Georgia Infantry was captured by the 2nd Pennsylvania Reserves.

Confederate fire finally slackened when the Federal assault column disintegrated into the woods to the north. The respite proved short-lived, however. Bullets began to fly among the ranks of the Georgians at the northernmost end of Archer's line, zinging in from front, left, and rear. The Georgians, sitting in a bland saddle between two higher knolls, quickly ascertained that they were nearly surrounded. The bedraggled figures pressing in from the woods to the north, and even from the rear, were Yankees after all. Some of the Georgians ran the gauntlet of fire into the safety of the woods; others, paralyzed by fear, stuck to the works.

After nearly fifteen minutes, Lieutenant Evan Woodward, the adjutant of the 2nd Pennsylvania Reserves, negotiated a surrender. The 19th Georgia turned over its battle flag even as many of the regiment's men tried to escape by running down the front face of the hill toward the rail line. Thirty years later, Woodward would receive the Medal of Honor for his deeds. It was the only set of colors captured by Federals during the entire battle.

Positioned on the line beyond the Georgians, the 14th Tennessee was next to fall. As they broke and ran, members of the 7th Tennessee, next in line, took such umbrage that their officers and men turned and fired on the fleeing men from their own state. The Pennsylvanians, too, took friendly fire. Fellow Keystoners, the 7th Pennsylvania Reserves, were positioned downhill in front of the Georgians; most of their fire went high, hitting men from the 2nd Pennsylvania Reserves.

"Ol' Jube," Brig. Gen. Jubal Early—Lee's "Bad Old Man"

69

Artillery on Prospect Hill along the Confederate position today.

Archer redeployed his battle line and called for help, which came pouring out of the woods to the west. Another of Jackson's division commanders, Brigadier General Jubal Early, had reacted to the pending disaster and sent one of his brigades straight into the action. Such a move, without orders from the by-the-book Jackson, might have cost Early his commission. "This was so serious an emergency that I determined to act upon it at once," Early later explained, "not withstanding the previous directions from General Jackson to hold my division in readiness for another purpose, and I accordingly ordered Atkinson to advance with his brigade."

Colonel Edmund Atkinson's six Georgia regiments swept onto the field, crying, "Here comes old Jubal!" and "Jubal's boys are always getting Hill out o' trouble!" Hill's earlier lament—that he'd get all the blame for the debacle instead of Jackson—was already coming true.

Meade's men, disorganized, unsupported, and running out of ammunition, had lost their steam, so Atkinson's strong counterattack sent them reeling. Lieutenant Colonel Samuel Jackson of the 11th Pennsylvania, the highest-ranking surviving officer on the scene, ordered the mixed Federal units into retreat.

**Confederate infantry
at Hamilton's Crossing.**

Early also sent men to plug the breakthrough at its
northern end, where a harried James Lane was barely
fending off Federal attacks on two fronts—from Meade's
Pennsylvanians scattered in the woods and Gibbons'
advancing men across Slaughter Pen Farm. Colonel James
A. Walker, leading this wing of Early's counterattack, first
had to maneuver around a slow-moving Confederate brigade
under the command of Brigadier General Elisha F. "Bull"
Paxton, which had inadvertently lumbered into the way. Once
past them, though, Walker's brigade easily outflanked the
Pennsylvanians and drove them from the field, back through
the woods, back to the rail line. Lane's men moved down from
the north and helped replug the gap. "It was a nasty time thar
for a bit," a Federal later said.

By 3:00 p.m., the fighting atop the hill was over. The
Union breakthrough was no more.

*   *   *

"I...will simply say my men went in <u>beautifully</u>, carried
everything before them, and drove the enemy for nearly
half a mile...." Meade later wrote to his wife. He had seen
the breakthrough, had known his men would need support
to exploit it, had pleaded for reinforcements that never got
ordered forward—had been the only Union officer anywhere
on the battlefield that day to taste success.

Unable to find Reynolds, Meade attempted to call on the
division of David Bell Birney. However, because Birney was
not in Meade's corps, let alone the same grand division, Birney
refused to accept orders from Meade or move to his assistance.
After two couriers failed to persuade him, the "ol' snapping
turtle" paid Birney a personal visit—and exploded on him.
"Meade was almost wild with rage as he saw the golden
opportunity slipping away from him," an observer reported.

A view from Prospect Hill across an area now obscured by trees that hide a modern industrial area.

His tone, said another, "almost makes the stones creep...."

"General, I assume the authority of ordering you up to the relief of my men," Meade growled at Birney, who complied—but by then, it was too late.

Surely this failure rests most squarely on Reynolds as corps commander. Instead of being at the ready to send reinforcements to exploit any success, Reynolds spent the battle riding along his artillery line suggesting to gunners how and where they should sight their pieces—a task already being ably overseen by his chief of artillery, Charles Wainwright. Reynolds acted the role of a major, not a major general.

More could have and should have been done by Franklin, as well. Convinced that his offensive was only in support of the assaults at Marye's Heights, he did not commit all the men he could have. Meade's 3,800 men had little real chance of besting Jackson's 40,000.

Nearly a century and a half would pass before historians would solve the puzzle of Franklin's December 13 confusion. On Burnside's map, the Old Richmond Road veered away from the Bowling Green Road and beelined straight toward Prospect Hill. So, when he ordered Franklin to be ready to make a quick movement down that road with his whole command, Burnside believed he was ordering Franklin to attack with everything he had. On Franklin's map, however, the Old Richmond Road did not run in the direction of Prospect Hill.

Meade's and Gibbon's assaults at Prospect Hill and the Slaughter Pen Farm were the only Union offensives to breach the Confederate line at Fredericksburg. Losses on both sides—5,000 Union, 4,000 Confederate—testify to the ferocity of the struggle. "All the men agree it was the warmest work the Reserves had ever encountered," Meade wrote.

Smithfield

"Jackson at Fredericksburg"—
Stonewall Jackson sits astride
his horse at the center of the
painting.

At Prospect Hill

After the war, James Lane would be among those pointing an accusatory finger at A. P. Hill. In a letter to Union historian Augustus Hamlin, Lane wrote: "The gap on my right was a great mistake & caused the gallant Gregg his life." Above the word "mistake," Lane wrote in "A. P. Hill's." There was no way Lane would ever cast blame for the mishap on Stonewall Jackson. Lane's North Carolinians accidentally shot Jackson at the battle of Chancellorsville—something for which he took more than his share of blame. The lifelong guilt Lane felt as a result ensured he would shift blame away from his fallen commander and thus help Hill's prophecy come true.

Yet Jackson was on the scene the entire time, supervising the action on Prospect Hill.

Prospect Hill was an unassuming 110-foot rise in the Spotsylvania county countryside in 1862. No house or structure stood atop it, nor was it cultivated at all. To the east, though, were the open fields of the Smithfield Plantation. When the fog lifted from the field in the late morning of December 13, Confederates had an excellent view of their foes arraying themselves for battle. Today, a heavy wood line blocks out a large industrial center and housing development to the front and front right.

Directly below the hill runs the rail line of the CSX. Two sets of tracks run today, but at the time of the battle, there was a single set owned and operated by the Richmond, Fredericksburg, and Potomac Railroad (R.F.&P.).

To the north, you have an excellent view up the Confederate line, occupied here by Archer's Brigade. A low rifle pit, made of earthworks and railroad ties, ran along the military crest of the ridge—a position just a few yards forward of the topographical crest. What looks like a low mound of earth had once been a trench two to four feet deep. (Feel free to walk along the Confederate line, but as you do, please do not walk on or over the earthworks, which damages them.)

Directly behind the infantry, the gunners of Reuben

L. Walker's battalion of artillery hunkered behind crescent-shaped earthworks called lunettes (a French word meaning "little moon").

After artillerists dug a lunette, they placed their cannon in the open space in the middle. The churned earth helped protect the gun crew and cannon. The rear of the lunette remained open, much like a half moon, so that the gun could be easily withdrawn if an enemy overran the position.

At the extreme north end of Prospect Hill, a wood line sheltered Maxcy Gregg's South Carolinians; that's where some of the Federals assaulting Prospect Hill emerged from. There's a saddle between two high spots along the Confederate line, too—the blind knoll gave the 19th Georgia so much grief when those Federals emerged.

The wood line juts out beyond the rail line, past a large pyramid, toward the open fields beyond. This is the point-of-woods that drew in the Federals as they attempted to relief from Confederate fire.

The large stone pyramid, known as the "Meade Pyramid," is not actually a monument to Meade or his Pennsylvania Reserves. It was the brainchild of the Confederate Memorial Literary Society (CMLS) and the former president of the R.F.&P., Major Edmund T. D. Myers. The CMLS had sought to place wooden signs along the tracks of Virginia railroads to mark the locations of Civil War battles. When they contacted the R.F.&P., Myers liked the idea so much he took it one step further. He sent one of his employees, John Rice, to Hollywood Cemetery in Richmond, Virginia, where a large pyramid had been erected to honor Confederate dead. Rice took measurements of that pyramid so that Meyers and the CMLS could construct one of their own.

In October 1897, Mrs. Eliza Pratt, who owned what was left of the Smithfield plantation, donated a small plot of land for construction of the memorial, which began in January 1898 and was concluded on March 31. It measures twenty-four feet tall and weighs four hundred tons. To this day, railroad passengers who glimpse the Meade Pyramid as they whiz by know they're passing through the Fredericksburg battlefield. Visitors who wish for a close-up view of the pyramid can follow a path down to the railroad tracks. (For your safety, however, do not cross the tracks to view the pyramid, which is in need of structural stabilization and is also a favorite spot for snakes to bask in the sun.)

It's also roughly along that route that Lieutenant Colonel Samuel Jackson led his mixed bag of units off the hill. Jackson's unit, the 11th Pennsylvania Reserves, sustained the highest number of casualties of any unit that fought on Prospect Hill: 211 of 300 men engaged fell killed wounded or missing. Jackson himself, though, survived the battle and the

The Meade Pyramid

war. Returning to Pittsburgh, he amassed a small fortune by investing in a trust company, becoming an influential Western Pennsylvanian. Jackson's grandson, too, was an influential Western Pennsylvanian: silver screen star Jimmy Stewart.

The woods on the west side of Prospect Hill were filled with two divisions—18,000 men—from Stonewall Jackson's Second corps. Walker's battalion also parked their ammunition chests, excess wagons, and horses just over the backside of the hill. With nothing to initially aim at, Federal artillerists tended to shoot high and long, missing Confederate gunners and but striking their teams of horses in the rear. So many horses were killed by the artillery fire that, after the battle, locals began calling this place "Dead Horse Hill."

Two walking tails lead from Prospect Hill. The first is the Hamilton's Crossing Trail, which begins at the dead-end of Lee Drive, to the right of the parking lot. The trail extends approximately one-half mile down to the southern base of Prospect Hill—the southern terminus of the Southern line.

The second trail from Prospect Hill begins in the rear of the parking area, where a few steps lead into the woods. This is the South Lee Drive Trail; it runs for 2.3 miles and is not a loop trail. The trail winds through the hollow where many of the horses were killed and through Jackson's reserve battle line, where soldiers dug an extensive trench system.

⟶ TO STOP 9

Follow Lee Drive 1.5 miles. On the right, you will see a small parking area for the Bernard's Cabin trailhead.

GPS Coordinates: N 38.25378 W 77.45960

Bernard's Cabins

CHAPTER TEN

Bernard's Cabin, also named Latimer's Knoll, was a key feature on the south end of the Fredericksburg battlefield. Looking east, over the interpretive markers you will see the northwestern corner of the Slaughter Pen Farm and the tracks of the modern CSX Railroad.

Throughout the December battle, this knoll provided a perfect artillery platform for Rebel gunners. Coupled with his guns at Prospect Hill to the south, Stonewall Jackson hoped to create a cross-fire with the guns at this position, enabling him to pour direct, indirect, plunging, and enfilading fire down any Federal assault column.

Captain Greenlee Davidson of the Letcher Artillery initially commanded the guns here. Davidson massed nine cannon on the high ground in support of Brigadier General James Lane's brigade to their front right. To their rear, Brigadier General William Dorsey Pender's brigade stood vigil. During the fight, Pender would be wounded, an observer recalled, "his left-hand hanging down and blood streaming down his fingers. A ball had gone through his arm between the bones." Pender dismissed it—"Oh, that is a trifle; no bone is broken."— and played a key role in rallying the Confederate defense during Gibbon's assault across the Slaughter Pen Farm.

Davidson's gunners, meanwhile, poured murderous fire into Gibbon's men. "My guns were double shotted with canister and we let them have it low," Davidson recalled. "The head of the column went down like wheat before the reaper. Another and another volley in quick succession completed the work. The Yankees broke, took to their heels and you never saw such a stampede."

Davidson's gunners were integral in deflating Union hopes on the south end of the field. They did their job so effectively, the young artillerist stated, that "[t]he grove of pines in my front is no longer entitled to the name. Many of the trees cut short off

Modern interpretive markers refer to the "Mannsfield Slave Cabins Trail," but historically, the small collection of slave dwellings was widely known as "Bernard's Cabins."

The settlement of slave cabins looked much like this collection of simple log huts.

and the trunks and branches are scattered in every direction."

Davidson's guns were later augmented by the five guns of Captain Joseph Latimer's artillery battalion. In all, fourteen pieces of artillery served the Confederacy well near Bernard's Cabin.

Prior to the war, Bernard's Cabin was a collection of four

The ruins of Mannsfield.

small, two-room, single-story double cabins that most likely housed some forty slaves owned by Arthur Bernard. Bernard owned seventy-seven slaves in all, and he used them to tend to his mansion, Mannsfield (built in 1766), and his 1,800-acre plantation. Also situated near the cabins was a stone-lined well, which served both slave and soldier.

In the middle of the battle's hottest artillery action, a Federal missile fell among the Confederate limber chests, striking one and igniting between 15 to 20 rounds that shot in all directions throughout the battery. The explosion was particularly hard on the wooden slave quarters According to Davidson, "The negro cabins are in ruins."

At Bernard's Cabins

A 0.9-mile trail loops through woods and open fields to the Bernard's Cabin site and back, taking you through the Confederate line to Davidson's and Latimer's gun position. Look closely to your left and right and you will make out the remains of numerous Confederate trench lines that were cut before the battle and throughout the winter of 1863.

While at the site of the cabins, look toward Shannon

Interpretive signs and a panoramic view await visitors who make the hike to the site.

Airport, which will be to your front left past the two interpretive markers. Shannon Airport denotes the extreme right flank of Reynolds' assault column. Behind the airport, along modern day Route 2/Route 17, sat idle men of the Union Sixth Corps. To your front right, you will notice the lines of the CSX and the open farm fields of the Slaughter Pen Farm. Gibbon's men would advance toward the rail line below you, held by Lane's Tar Heels.

Davidson's men would have angled their guns to fire solid shot, case shot, and canister into the flank of Gibbon's men as they came across the open assault plain. Gibbon's survivors would have entered the woods below you and to your right, filling the woods with Federals. From your rear, the men of Dorsey Pender's North Carolina brigade approached to help secure the Confederate guns and launch counterattacks back down to the railroad.

⟶ TO STOP 10

Follow Lee Drive 0.6 miles to the stop sign at Landsdowne Road. Cross over Landsdowne Road and follow Lee Drive 2.5 miles. On your left will be the parking area for Lee Hill. *On the Park Service's driving tour, this is tour stop three, Lee's Hill.*

GPS Coordinates: N 38° 28648 W 77° 47533

Confederates moved across the field, beyond the trees in the upper-right corner, to meet Gibbon's attack. Later, Jackson looked to make a counterattack across the same ground.

Telegraph Hill

CHAPTER ELEVEN

From his command post atop Telegraph Hill, Robert E. Lee had watched the spectacle of war unfold before him. The blue host, materializing out of the morning's last wisps of fog, marching in perfect order westward from the Bowling Green Road, flags unfurled, officers atop horseback—it all looked so martial, so magnificent.

"It is well that war is so terrible," the Confederate commander remarked, "or we should grow too fond of it."

Earlier that morning, the Southern high command had congregated at Lee's headquarters, which offered an especially impressive view to the south, toward the right end of Longstreet's Corps and most of Jackson's Corps. To the north, the generals could see the southern end of Fredericksburg and some of the open fields the stretched up from the city toward the base of Marye's Heights, although the heights themselves blocked part of the view.

Jackson, normally dust-covered and road-ragged, showed up at the meeting wearing a new uniform coat given to him by cavalryman J.E.B. Stuart and a new gold-braided hat sent to him by his wife. "As he dismounted we broke into astonished smiles," one of Longstreet's staffers said. "We had never seen the like before, and gave him our congratulations on his really fine appearance." Jackson seemed appreciative, if a little self-conscious of the attention.

"General," Longstreet gibed, keeping in the spirit of the meeting's light mood, "do not all those multitudes of Federals frighten you?"

"We shall see very soon whether I shall not frighten them," Jackson replied, ready as ever for business.

"What are you going to do with all those people over there?" Longstreet asked.

"Sir, we will give them the bayonet."

Shortly thereafter, Lee went with Jackson, Stuart, and Hill to inspect the south part of the line—noticing and approving

A pair of artillery pieces, a small monument, and an exhibit shelter crown Telegraph Hill—rechristened "Lee Hill" after the battle because the Confederate commander made his headquarters there.

From the top of Telegraph Hill, Lee and Longstreet watched the spectacle of battle unfold before them. "It is well that war is so terrible," Lee said, "or we should grow too fond of it."

the gap in Hill's line across the swamp en route. By the time the battle began in earnest, Lee had returned to his perch atop the hill. His hands-off approach to the battle allowed both Longstreet and Jackson, who knew their tasks well and were ready for most contingencies, to conduct their own affairs. Messengers from both wings came in to the army's nerve center with updates, but Lee spent much of the day as a spectator.

Heavy cannon, including a Southern-made 30-pounder Parrott gun, sat atop the crest of Telegraph Hill and launched enfilading fire against Federals assaulting the southern end of Marye's Heights. At one point, the Union Ninth Corps attempted to use an unfinished rail to flank the heights, but the guns on Telegraph Hill fired down the rail cut, cutting short the Ninth Corps' move. "The long cut, the moving mass, the lanes mowed through it, reminded me of wanton boys dealing death to hosts of ants as they constantly advance, unchecked by the ever-increasing pile of dead comrades," a gunner said. Later in the day, men of the Union Fifth Corps felt the wrath of the Telegraph Hill guns, too.

In 1862, Lee had an unobscured view toward downtown Fredericksburg, although the crest of Marye's Heights hid much of the action on the slope of the heights from Lee's view. To the south, the plains of the Slaughter Pen Farm were in clear sight. Today, a far-off church steeple—a little speck of white—is about the only thing visible, especially with summer foliage crowding in on the view.

As advantageous as the position was for Lee's cannoneers, having an artillery position so close to headquarters proved especially hazardous because artillery attracts counter-battery fire. One such incoming shell planted itself in an earthwork beside Lee; had it exploded, it surely would have killed or maimed the Confederate commander. Instead, it turned out to be a dud. Later in the action, the 30-pounder Parrott gun exploded as it was being fired. "[T]he entire forepart of the gun…whent whirling over and over, down the hill, in front of us. Small portions flew to each side, and the entire rear took the back track for the woods," one artillerist recalled. Lee nor Longstreet, who were there at the time, escaped injury, as did the artillerists.

After the December battle, Lee moved his headquarters from Telegraph Hill to the Cox house, some two miles distant along Mine Road. Lee nonetheless left behind an indelible mark on the hill that now bears his name.

Another of Smith's markers sits atop Lee Hill, marking the spot of the commander's HQ.

At Telegraph Hill

On the morning of the battle, artillerist David McIntosh recounted the scene from the top of Telegraph Hill:

> *Our expectations were excited all the more from the fact that a heavy fog hung over the plain concealing it from our view. But though we could not see through the fog, there was no lack of ominous sounds to indicate what was going on. The heavy rumble of artillery and ordnance wagons, the bugle calls, and the noise of many bands of music filled the air, and we knew full well what it all meant. When the mist lifted about ten o'clock, a gorgeous panorama was spread out*

The path to the top of Telegraph Hill is moderately steep and takes between seven and ten minutes to climb.

before us…. As far as the eye could see, back towards the river, and stretching up towards Fredericksburg, the vast plain was filled with moving masses of men, rapidly deploying and forming alignments into what appeared to be three lines of battle, and here and there large gaps in the lines being filled with artillery, while moving about and adding more life and color to the scene were squadrons of cavalry. Back of it all the Stafford Heights stood out crowned with heavy Parrotts and siege pieces, which had not waited for the mist to lift before they began throwing their heavy missiles and feeling our position. No grander military spectacle was ever presented to human view….

Telegraph Hill, two-hundred and forty-three feet high, is situated between Willis Hill, which is the southern terminus of Marye's Heights, and the northern slope of Howison Hill. It sits near the center of the Confederates' strong defensive position.

Federals never actually assaulted the hill during the battle of Fredericksburg, although Brigadier General Joseph Kershaw's South Carolina brigade had been posted along the base in case of just such an eventuality. It wouldn't be until the following May, during the battle of Second Fredericksburg—part of the Chancellorsville campaign—that Federal troops would storm and take the hill, which was used at the time as a headquarters by Confederate Brigadier General William Barksdale.

A switchback trail leads to the top of the hill. During the winter and early spring when the trees are stripped of their leaves, a narrow viewshed offers a hint of the panoramic perspective that Lee and his staff officers had from their headquarters. A small exhibit shelter houses exhibits focused on Second Fredericksburg.

Telegraph Hill wasn't the only Confederate artillery position along Lee Drive. At Howison Hill, tucked behind a large lunette, visitors can see a 30-pounder Parrott gun —an artillery piece typically used as a seige gun and so not usually found on battlefields.

➡ TO STOP 11

Turn left out of the parking area and follow Lee Drive 0.1 miles to the intersection of Lee Drive and Route 1/Lafayette Boulevard. Turn right onto Lafayette Boulevard and follow it for 0.2 miles. Continue through the intersection for 0.4 miles and turn left into the battlefield visitor center and park in the rear of the building. *On the Park Service's driving tour, this is tour stop one, "Fredericksburg Battlefield Visitor Center."*

GPS Coordinates: N 38° 29379 W 77°.46740

Lee Drive

The Sunken Road

CHAPTER TWELVE

As Ambrose Burnside's main assault finally began on the south end of the field, his diversionary assaults against Marye's Heights—the assaults history would ultimately remember and condemn him for—also went forward. Thirty thousand soldiers would ultimately make their way from the city of Fredericksburg uphill across mostly open ground against a strongly fortified Confederate position.

Leading the way out of the city was the division of Brigadier General William French, part of Couch's Second Corps in Sumner's Right Grand Division. Known as "Blinky" because of an uncontrollable tendency to blink and squint, French had driven Stonewall Jackson to resign from the old army years earlier because of a personality clash between the two. Today, he'd clash not against his old nemesis but against Longstreet, ensconced with his men atop Marye's Heights.

Fredericksburg might have triggered déjà vu among French's men. Two months earlier at Antietam, they had been part of an assault column that charged a sunken road that Confederates had been using as a fortified rifle pit. Here again they faced a similar task. At Antietam, when Federals finally did break through, trapped Confederates had no place to run, and Federals shot them down so thickly that their bodies carpeted the ditch from one side to another, eventually earning the name "Bloody Lane." Here, they could only hope for similar results.

The topography did not favor the Federals. The attack plain consisted of an open expanse, 900 yards across, that gently inclined toward Marye's Heights, 130 feet above sea level. To the north, Gordon's Marsh hemmed them in; to the south, an unfinished railroad cut and Hazel Run confined them likewise. In the path forward, four fences bisected the fields. A millrace, fifteen feet wide by five feet deep, with three feet of standing water in the bottom, also bisected the field. Three bridges crossed the canal, but Confederates had taken up the wooden

As the most famous part of the Fredericksburg Battlefield, the area around the Battlefield Visitor Center is home to some of the battlefield's most iconic features: the Stone Wall, the Sunken Road, the Innis House, and the Kirkland Memorial.

A view of Marye's Heights from Federal Hill.

Brig. Gen. Thomas Cobb

planks from the bridges, although they left the iron support runners, wide enough to be crossed like a balance beam by Union soldiers—perfect targets for snipers and artillerists.

Should the Federals cross that terrain, Brigadier General Thomas R. R. Cobb's brigade of Georgians, posted along the Telegraph Road behind a stone wall, waited to meet them.

Cobb, known by many as the Thomas Jefferson of the Confederacy, was a firebrand lawyer from the state of Georgia who ardently defended states' rights and the institution of slavery. After helping to draft the Confederate Constitution, he chose to forgo politics in favor of raising a mixed regiment of infantry, cavalry, and artillery known as Cobb's Legion. On November 1, 1862, he received his brigadier general's star and, when he arrived at Fredericksburg, was ordered to hold the Telegraph Road, which ran just below the crest of Marye's Heights.

Cobb made his headquarters in the home of Martha Stephens while his men tucked into the road and fortified the small intersection beside the Innis House. They cleared their fields of fire and placed white pieces of wood in the open plain to mark yardage so they would know when to open fire effectively. "I think my brigade can whip ten thousand of them attacking us in front," Cobb boasted. "We have a magnificent position, the best perhaps on the line."

Confederate artillerists at the very crest of the hill—the vaunted Washington Artillery of New Orleans, Louisiana— also pre-sighted the open plain. The artillerists had infantry support from the North Carolina brigade of Brigadier General John Rogers Cooke, the brother-in-law of Jeb Stuart and son of Union cavalryman Phillip St. George Cooke.

As French's men, shielded by the safety of the city, looked ahead at what awaited them, dreading for the order that

The attack on Marye's Heights.

would send them forward, French tried to keep their spirits up. "Cheer up my hearties, cheer up!" he called. "This is something we all must get used to! Remember, this brigade has never been whipped—don't let it get whipped today!"

Just before 11:00 a.m., Sumner sent the order to Couch; Couch sent the order to French; French sent the order to his three brigade commanders: "Forward!"

"At last the Federal line is formed, and appears above the ridge and advances," a member of the Washington Artillery said:

> *What a magnificent sight it is! We have never witnessed such a battle-array before; long lines following one another.... It seemed like some huge blue serpent about to encompass and crush us in its folds, their musket-barrels gleaming brightly in the sunlight, their gay colors fluttering in the breeze. The lines advance at the double quick, and the alignments are beautifully kept. The board fences enclosing the gardens fall like walls of mere paper. Then the loud, full voice of Col Walton rings out, ' 'tention! Commence fir-i-ing!!' and instantly the edge of Marye's Hill is fringed with flame. The dreadful work of the Washington Artillery has begun.*

Maj. Gen. William "Blinky" French

Some of the lead Union units hoped to dash across the open field and race uphill behind the Confederate skirmish line, using the skirmishers as human shields, assuming the Confederates would never willingly fire on their own men. The Confederates didn't have to. The fields were muddied from melted snow in the days leading to battle. Federals found it too slippery to catch up with their human shields.

"[O]ur men were killed very fast and we were doing no good," a Connecticut private said.

The terrain's other obstructions proved problematic, too. "The fences had to be pushed or cut down, and there were several extremely bad bogs, or holes, taking men in half leg

The canal ditch then and now.

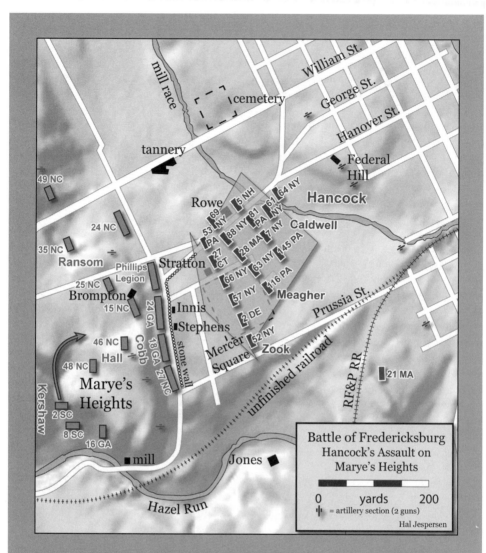

ATTACK OF THE IRISH BRIGADE—Seven full Federal assaults attempted to break the Marye's Heights line. One of the most iconic units in the Federal assault, Brigadier General Thomas F. Meagher's Irish Brigade, tested their mettle against the heights during the second major Federal assault, commanded by Maj. Gen. Winfield Scott Hancock. Like their brethren before and after, they never touched the stone wall or made it into the sunken road.

deep," a Union officer said.

Behind the stone wall, Cobb watched and waited. As the Federals pushed closer through the hail of artillery, Cobb let them get one-hundred yards away—then he dropped his hat, and the Confederates fired for ten continuous minutes. Cobb finally called for a brief ceasefire to allow the smoke to rise from the field. "You can't imagine what a horrible spectacle I witnessed," a Georgian later said. "I saw hundreds of men lying dead, shot in all parts some with their heads, hands, legs arms, etc. shot off, and mangled in all manner and shapes. The ground resembled an immense hog pen and them all killed...." No Federal soldier had made it any closer than fifty yards.

*   *   *

Brig. Gen. Thomas Meagher

More Federals made their way to the front: the fine division of the brave and capable Brigadier General Winfield Scott Hancock. Like French's men, they had assaulted the Bloody Lane at Antietam where they, too, sustained heavy casualties.

Colonel Samuel Zook's brigade led the assault. "[T]he fire was so heavy, and the shells were bursting in such numbers that I involuntarily turned my head as you would in a rain storm," said one of Zook's officers.

After Zook's advance stalled, Hancock sent in his next brigade, perhaps the most famous Federal unit to fight on the battlefield: the 1,500 men of the Irish Brigade, mainly immigrant Sons of Erin from New York, Massachusetts, and Pennsylvania. The brigade's regiments normally carried both the United States flag and a green Irish flag into action, but on December 13th, only the 28th Massachusetts had their Irish flag. The rest of the brigade's flags had been so badly damaged in the 1862 campaigns that they had been sent to New York for repair and replacement. As a substitute, the man leading the Irish Brigade into action, Brigadier General Thomas F. Meagher, urged his men to tuck sprigs of boxwood into their hats.

When the Irishmen took to the field, they had two tasks. First, they had to leapfrog forward through the killing fields past Zook's brigade; second, they had to attack with enough

Federal troops mass for another assault. As they swept up the hill, comrades already pinned down in the field grabbed at their legs, begging them not to go forward, breaking their momentum.

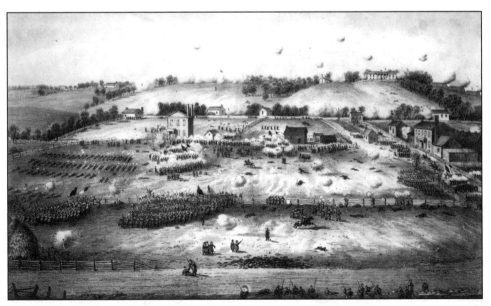

vigor to provide cover for the survivors of French's division, now pinned down behind a shallow swale, to retreat for safety. The Irishmen "charged the enemy, who were well protected behind a stone wall, and received a murderous fire from both

musketry ad artillery," one of them recalled in a letter home. Wounded and unwounded survivors of the previous waves of attack sprawled on the ground, and dead were strewn everywhere, making advance difficult. Meagher's men nonetheless made it to within approximately forty yards of the wall and, from their exposed position, blasted away. A wall of lead from the Georgians and North Carolinians in the road and on the heights stopped the advance cold. By the end of the fighting, one third of the Irish—545 of 1,500 men—fell as casualties.

The Irish Brigade got about this far—about forty yards— from the Stone Wall.

Watching from the cupola of the city courthouse, Second Corps commander Darius Couch understood the futility of the attacks. "I had never before seen fighting like that, nothing approaching it in terrible uproar and destruction," he later said.

There was no cheering on the part of the men, but a stubborn determination to obey orders and do their duty. As they charged the artillery fire would break their formation and they would get mixed; then they would close up, go forward, receive the withering infantry fire, and those who were able would run to the houses and fight as best they could; and then the next brigade coming up in succession would do its duty and melt like snow coming down on warm ground.

At 1:45 p.m., Couch signaled back across the river: "It is only murder now."

But Burnside could not call off the attacks. For one thing, with so many men stranded on the field, he needed to keep up pressure to prevent any Confederate counterattack. More importantly, he needed to continue the diversion so that Lee wouldn't shift troops to the south end of the field where Franklin was by now, he assumed, capturing Prospect Hill. Because Franklin failed to keep Burnside in the loop, the army commander had no way of knowing that action in the southern sector had reached its crescendo and that, even now, Meade's un-reinforced men were getting turned back. Although things at Marye's Heights looked grim, Burnside continued the assaults there to support an attack at the far end of the field that was, unbeknownst to him, no longer happening.

And so next in: the division of Brigadier General Oliver Otis Howard. Two of his three brigades went forward but the third, that of Brigadier General Alfred Sully, remained in reserve. "I was not going to murder my men, and it would be

As one of the few structures in the open plain between the city and the stone wall, the Stratton House along Mercer Street offered crucial protection for Federal soldiers unable to retreat back to safety. "I found the brick house packed with men," said Darius Couch; "and behind it the dead and the living were as thick as they could be crowded together. The dead were rolled out for shelter, and the dead horses were used for breastworks."

nothing less than murder to have sent them there," Sully said. Survivors of the assault seemed to bear out his prediction. "We received such a withering, deadly fire from the enemy that it was impossible to get more than half way across that open ground, and we were compelled to fall back and seek cover," one of them said. "It seemed as if the earth had opened up and swallowed whole regiments at a time."

The next Union assaults attempted to flank the Sunken Road. Men moved out of the city north of Hanover Street, straight into Gordon's Marsh, where the attacks literally and figuratively bogged down. With that idea a failure, Federals looked to the other end of the Sunken Road, where they tried to advance under the cover of an unfinished railroad cut. Men of the Union Ninth Corps leapt from the cut, taking the Confederates by surprise, but suddenly concentrated artillery fire rained down from the heights and Telegraph Hill, devastating that assault.

"Great gaps are torn in the ranks; men are falling all around us," a Federal soldier said; "another and another line of battle come charging up behind mingling their forces with ours; we struggle towards that stone wall that is belching out its hail of iron and fire; but all in vain, we cannot reach it."

In total, seven waves of Federal troops threw themselves against the Stone Wall.

Maj. Gen. Darius Couch

*   *   *

Confederates, snug as they were behind their wall, were having problems of their own. Between French's assault and Hancock's, Cobb had been standing in the road, discussing the battle with John Rogers Cooke. Shortly after they wrapped up their conversation, a Federal shell screamed into the road and

Plumes of smoke from cannons, musketfire, and burning buildings rose over the city.

exploded, sending shrapnel into Cobb's left leg and severing his femoral artery. "I am only wounded, boys," Cobb told his men. "Hold your ground like brave men." Confederates evacuated Cobb to a field hospital behind Telegraph Hill, where he bled to death within the hour.

Command devolved to Cooke, but a spent bullet cracked his skull, knocking him out of the fight. He would survive the battle —it was just one of five wounds he sustained in the war—but his absence left a leadership vacuum.

Not that the enlisted men felt so concerned about that as they did a more pressing issue: they had too many targets and not enough ammunition. "I thought we would have to come to charge bayonets on them, but just in the 'nick' of time here came the old 2nd S.C. Vols. like so many wild Indians," one Confederate wrote in a letter home. "I tell you I felt good, for we had shot away 70 rounds of cartridges & the Yankies were still coming."

To solve the resupply issue, Longstreet shifted entire brigades into the Sunken Road as support, and they all brought with them full boxes of ammunition. As the day wore on, North Carolinians, South Carolinians, and Virginians all joined Cobb's Georgians. To get to the road, though, Confederates had to come down the bald face of Marye's Heights, which subjected them to a storm of Union lead.

A modern view of the Stone Wall.

As things got more crowded in the Sunken Road, men in the back loaded weapons and passed them to marksmen in the

"A chicken could not live on that field when we open up on it," a Confederate artillerist said.

front, who passed spent rifles back in exchange. One Georgian claimed that he fired over 500 rounds that day. Other units lined up four deep, and after the man in the front rank fired, he would step to the back of the line and begin to reload as the second man in line stepped to the front and fire. Thus, Confederates kept up a constant ring of fire.

"All that day we watched the fruitless charges, with their fearful slaughter, until we were sick at heart," a Confederate private later said. "What chance had flesh and blood to carry by storm such a position, garrisoned too as it was with veteran soldiers?

*   *   *

Burnside launched more assaults against this "Gibraltar of the South." Exhausting his supply of troops from Sumner's Right Grand Division, he called on men from Joseph Hooker's Center Grand Division.

In one of the most dramatic assaults of the day, Brigadier General Andrew A. Humphreys looked to take the position by bayonet. Humphreys was one of the only general officers to actually ride onto the battlefield on horseback, and he challenged his seven staff officers to ride out, as well. Five of the seven of them were wounded or unhorsed, including the general's own son, while Humphreys himself lost two horses and a hat. His men drove to within fifty yards of the wall before the galling fire repelled them. The Pennsylvanians in Humphreys's division were felled by the dozens.

At the far end of the stone wall, just as dusk settled in,

A historic view of the Sunken Road and Stone Wall, with the Innis House in the middle distance.

The Innis House was used by Brig. Gen. Thomas Cobb as his headquarters before his mortal wounding. Bullet holes scar the building on both sides— including the side facing away from the advancing Federals because of a friendly-fire incident. North Carolinians on the heights across the street fired too low when deployed in a saddle of the hill, striking the home near the front door— and striking some Georgians stationed there in the back.

Brig. Gen. Andrew A. Humphries

Colonel Rush C. Hawkins of Brigadier General George Getty's brigade tried a bayonet charge of his own. Like the Ninth Corps soldiers earlier in the day, they advanced along the unfinished railroad cut, but the gloaming covered their approach. "We sprang to our feet, and with arms at a charge we rushed on, hallooing at the top of our voices," a New Jerseyman recalled. "I glanced to the rear, and not a man of the regiment was wavering." However, their shout gave away their position. "On ascending the top of a hill, the rebels poured a volley into our ranks," he said. A far-off observer watched the resultant light show. "I could not hear the guns but could see the flash and the wavering of the lines. Sometimes there was a solid sheet of flame but for the most part, twinkle, twinkle, twinkle, like sparks when a fire is stirred—rapid as thought. About 20 pieces of artillery poured an enfilading fire into our ranks. The shells burst right among them." Only full darkness brought an end to the fight.

The battle of Fredericksburg was over.

French...Hancock...Howard...Sturgis...Griffin...Humphreys...Hawkins. By the end of the day, Burnside's army had made seven major assaults against the heights, yet not a single Federal soldier touched the wall. Nearly 8,000 of them fell as casualties in front of the stone wall, compared to fewer than 1,000 Confederate casualties.

"[W]e could but wonder what delusions, what forlorn hope could possess the breast or brain of the opposing commander, that should lead him to order a continued repetition of the disastrous repulses," Confederate Brigadier General Lafayette McLaws later said.

The battle, said one Confederate, was "the very saturnalia of death."

Along the Sunken Road

With a neighborhood now filling the once-open nine-hundred-yard expanse between the stone wall and downtown Fredericksburg, it's hard to visualize the wartime killing fields.

For portions of its length, the Sunken Road had stone retaining walls running along both sides.

Where once Colonel Joshua Lawrence Chamberlain's 20th Maine spent the night pinned down on the battlefield, for instance, one can now buy a memorial Slurpee.

Very few structures dotted that no-man's land. The brick Stratton House and the wooden Sisson Store both sat 196 yards from the wall. Along the Sunken Road itself was the Hall House (where the visitor center sits today), the Stephens House, the Innis House, and Ebert Store.

The Innis House, in fact, survived two battles here and remained a private residence until January 1970, when the

The innis house, circa the 1960s, prior to its purchase by the Park Service.

Martha Stephens remains buried in her family plot, marked by a stone urn (below). The outline of her foundation and a recreated well are all that are left of her home (bottom). According to local tradition, Stephens stayed in her house during the battle and tended to wounded soldiers.

NPS purchased it for $36,600 from Dr. and Mrs. Carter Redd Rowe. By the time of the purchase, a front porch with a swing had been added, as well as a room off of the back of the home. A large television antenna adorned the roof. During a 1970's restoration, layers of old wallpaper were stripped from the interior, and old siding was removed from the exterior. The restoration revealed fifty-two bullet and shell holes throughout the home. On occasion, the Park Service opens the Innis House for tours.

Martha Stephens, who owned both the Innis and Stephens houses at the time of the battle, ran an illegal bar out of the Stephens House. One archeological dig along the Sunken Road located her trash pit, filled with oyster shells and champagne bottles. The battle necessitated a halt in business, but after the war, she regaled customers with tales of the fight: she stayed in her home, she claimed, and tended to wounded Confederates. To this day, her claims remain unsubstantiated,

The Telegraph Road, circa the 1880s, near the bend by Sisson's Store.

though. When interested patrons inquired about the hundreds of bullet holes that riddled her clapboard home, she sometimes offered to sell pieces of the house for fifty cents or a dollar. One piece of her home made it all the way to Chicago, where it was displayed in a museum.

Another small house once stood on the open attack plain itself—the modest Jennings House, which stood along modern-day Lafayette Boulevard where a Captain Dee's now stands. Expansion of the city threatened the Jennings House, which was moved to its current location across from the visitor center's parking lot for RVs and busses.

Also on the attack plain, just east of the visitor center, sat the old Fredericksburg Fairgrounds, Mercer Square, former home of one of the oldest agricultural fairs in the nation. The ten-acre fairground was enclosed by a wooden fence. In the war's early days, Confederates had trained units there. Just prior to the battle, Confederates returned to the fairgrounds, this time to rip down part of the fencing on the western side. They left the fence standing on the eastern side, though, so that when Federals approached it, they would either have to kick it down or go around. Either way, it would slow the advancing columns.

The restored road today.

The other major feature of the landscape was a stone wall that paralleled part of the Telegraph Road as it ran just below the crest of the heights. The Telegraph Road was the I-95 of its day. It ran north fifty miles to Washington D.C. and south fifty-five miles to Richmond. The Sunken Road remained an active road until 2004, when the city of Fredericksburg turned its care over to the NPS, which finally closed it and undertook a $580,000 restoration project. Today, the road now looks similar to its wartime appearance, although the road

base itself would have been more dirt than gravel.

Along this portion of the road sat a sturdy wall made of Aquia stone. The quarry, now extinct, furnished the same rock used to build many of the original government buildings in Washington D.C. The wall along the road was most likely used as a privacy fence to keep travelers out of the yards of the residents. Much of the wall was taken in postwar years by locals who used the stones for construction and by travelers who wanted a souvenir. One piece of the wall ended up as part of the state science museum of West Virginia; it's labeled and near the outside entrance to the building.

In order to restore some semblance of the battlefield's wartime appearance, the Civilian Conservation Corps rebuilt a portion of the stone wall in the 1930s, shortly after the park was first established. The next two portions of the wall are the most recent additions, built between 2004-05 as part of the road restoration project. Utilizing digitized pictures and archeological evidence, the Park Service was able to accurately re-create what the wall looked like, including its height and depth.

One original portion of the wall still remains, however, and it's along the only portion of the road that was actually sunken, directly below Brompton. There, the wall acts as a retaining wall for the earth to the east.

Most of the monuments on the Fredericksburg battlefield are clustered along this area. One of the oldest of those monuments is the marker for Thomas Cobb. Placed by his family in the late 1880's, the monument marks the approximate site of the young general's wounding. During the battle, Confederates along much of the road and on the

For $1.00 per day, men of the C.C.C. built the low stone wall, as well as the visitor center and carriage house, which today houses the park's bookstore.

The swale where so many Federals took shelter can best be seen looking down Mercer Street. The parked cars along the side of the road accentuate the dip.

On December 14, 1862, 19-year-old Sergeant Richard Kirkland of South Carolina loaded himself up with canteens filled from the well of Martha Stephens' house and jumped the wall, taking water to wounded and dying Federals on the field. For his act of compassion, he would earn the nickname "The Angle of Marye's Heights." The memorial for Kirkland was designed by Felix DeWeldon, the sculptor of the Iwo Jima Memorial in Arlington National Cemetery. DeWeldon produced the Kirkland Memorial for $25,000. It was dedicated on September 29, 1965.

heights above could see clearly into the city. One of the homes that sat on the city's edge, Federal Hill, had once belonged to Cobb's mother. "Tell Ma my camp is now on the hills immediately in the rear and west of old 'Federal Hill,'" Cobb wrote in a letter to his wife. "I can see the house plainly about one mile and a half distant, there being a level plain between it and my Hd. Qrs." He would be mortally wounded in sight of his mother's old homestead.

Approximately thirty feet across the road from the Cobb monument is a monument to Martha Stephens. The small stone was placed on December 18, 1917, by the United Daughters of the Confederacy and one of Stephens's biggest "fans," Judge John Goolrick. "Here Lived Mrs. Martha Stevens Friend of the Confederate Soldier, 1861-1865 U.D.C." it reads. (It should be noted that Stephens had three different aliases, so the spelling of Stephens differs from time to time.)

The largest monument on this sector of the battlefield is to Sergeant Richard Rowland Kirkland of the 2nd South Carolina Infantry. (His story is told in the epilogue.)

The NPS restoration of the Sunken Road also included a trail that leads across the crest of Marye's Heights. A blacktop access road, with a large brown gate, offers access to the heights. A large white home that sits on the heights was not there at the time of the battle; a former Confederate artillery officer, Charles Richardson, built it there in the 1890's. Later, the home served as part of Montfort Academy, which closed in 1996. Today, the home and land is owned by the NPS, but the home is not open to visitors.

From Marye's Heights, where cannons now mark the former positions of the Washington Artillery, one can still make out the spires of the city. Set back from the crest is a small brick-walled cemetery that belonged to the Willis family, for whom Willis Hill is named.

"War So Terrible..."

CHAPTER THIRTEEN

Despite the carnage of December 13, Ambrose Burnside still thought he could find victory at Fredericksburg. He planned to resume the assaults against the stone wall in the morning, despite protestations from his subordinates, and cut orders to that effect. He would personally lead the charge at the head of his old Ninth Corps, whose deep loyalty to him would inspire them to follow.

Confederates captured one of Burnside's couriers carrying a copy of the order. According to Longstreet, when Lee learned of Burnside's plans, he sent orders of his own "to improve defenses and prepare for the next day in ammunition, water, and rations, under conviction that the battle of next day, if made as ordered, would be the last of the Army of the Potomac."

Burnside's staff suspected the same result. By morning, they finally persuaded the army commander to change his mind. A teary-eyed Burnside, burning with frustration, humiliation, anger, and sorrow, called off the attack.

And so the day passed with Union soldiers, trapped behind a small swale in the field and behind barriers made from the corpses of their slain comrades, trading potshots with Confederates hunkered down behind the stone wall.

That night, the Northern Lights flashed across the sky—a rare thing so far south. "[T]he heavens were hanging out banners and streamers and setting off fireworks in honor of our victory," one Confederate said. Federals saw it as God honoring the brave sacrifice of their fallen comrades. Later that night, a storm blew in and blotted out the stars and moon. Under the thick darkness, Burnside ordered a withdrawal, and his army slipped back to the far side of the Rappahannock. "There is something, certainly not courage breeding, in a such a night and amid such scenes," a Pennsylvanian said.

Fredericksburg was in ruins—"a continuous charnel-house," a newspaper correspondent wrote. "Death, nothing but death everywhere; great masses of bodies tossed out of the churches as the sufferers expired; layers of corpses stretched in the balconies of houses as though taking a <u>siesta</u>. In one yard a surgeon's block for operating was still standing, and, more appalling to look

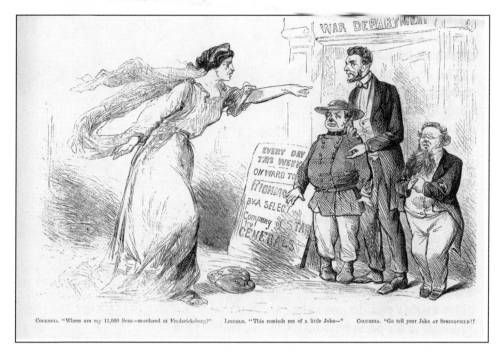

Columbia. "Where are my 15,000 Sons—murdered at Fredericksburg?"   Lincoln. "This reminds me of a little Joke—"   Columbia. "Go tell your Joke at Springfield!"

The press savaged Lincoln for another embarrassing defeat.

at even than the bodies of the dead, piles of arms and legs, amputated as soon as their owners had been carried off the field, were heaped in a corner. There were said to be houses literally crammed with the dead...."

One-thousand two-hundred and eighty-four Northerners died in the battle; nine-thousand six-hundred were wounded; one-thousand seven-hundred and sixty-nine were captured or missing—a total of 12,653 Union casualties. Six-hundred and eight Southerners were killed; four-thousand one-hundred and sixteen were wounded; six-hundred and fifty-three were captured or missing—a total of 5,377 Confederate casualties. It was the most lopsided defeat the Army of the Potomac suffered during the war.

Lee saw few fruits of victory, overwhelming as it was, because he gained no strategic advantage from it. He could not counterattack, else his men would have to expose themselves across the very killing fields that had made the Federals so susceptible. He could not push the Federals off the far banks of the Rappahannock. He contented himself to settle into position for the winter and await the spring campaign season.

Burnside was not so content. Still facing tremendous political pressure from Lincoln, especially after the Emancipation Proclamation went into effect January 1, he looked for another way to get at Lee. On January 20, 1863, he sent the bulk of his army on a wide flanking maneuver westward with the intent of circling down on Lee from behind. Heavy rains quickly mired the maneuver, which became known as the Mud March. "Burnside stuck in the mud," Confederates painted on a barn roof. Burnside, defeated this time by weather, called off the advance.

The Mud March: "The whole country was a river of mud," complained one soldier.

The Mud March, coupled with political maneuverings by several of his subordinates, proved Burnside's undoing. "The Army of the Potomac is no more an army," a Federal officer said. "Its patriotism has oozed out through the pores opened by the imbecility of its leaders, and the fatigues and disappointments of a fruitless campaign."

On January 26, Lincoln reassigned Burnside back to command of his old Ninth Corps and replaced him with "Fighting Joe" Hooker.

Chancellorsville awaited.

* * *

"What a bloody, one-sided battle this was," a Federal soldier complained in the wake of the December battle. "It was simply murder, and the whole army is mad about it. We are no fools! We can see when we have a chance; here we had none."

Another came to a similar epiphany while pinned down on the field in front of the stone wall. "I wondered while I lay there how it all came about that these thousands of men in broad daylight were trying their best to kill each other," he recalled. "Just then there was no romance, no glorious pomp, nothing but disgust for the genius who planned so frightful a slaughter."

That "genius," Ambrose Burnside, is still condemned by history for sending his men into such slaughter—but such condemnation reflects an incomplete understanding of the battle. Lincoln himself deserves as much of the blame. The administration's political pressure, in an effort to give the Emancipation Proclamation real strength, backed Burnside against the river. Coupled with Halleck's bungle, Burnside's choices got fewer and fewer as days ticked by until he had nothing but poor choices. It's no wonder modern students of the war can see how Burnside's folly looks preordained.

While the resolve of Confederate soldiers at Fredericksburg cannot be overestimated, Confederate partisans tend to overemphasize Lee's leadership. Lee knew he held a powerful

Former slaves hired by the Federal burial commission disinterred the dead from the battlefield for reburial in the national cemetery.

advantage in terrain, which did most of the work for him, yet he also approved the gap in A. P. Hill's line, which allowed that terrain to work against his army. While Stonewall Jackson's men tenaciously plugged the gap thanks to Jubal Early's initiative, things might have been much different had more Federals than just Meade's gone flooding into that gap. Confederates have Franklin's befuddlement to thank as much as Lee's generalship.

The two armies settled into winter quarters, making the Rappahannock the front line of the war for another five months. That, perhaps, is the most significant implication of the battle, for the Rappahannock became the *de facto* front line of emancipation. Beginning with the arrival of the Union army in the area in the spring of 1862 and continuing through its occupation of Falmouth and Stafford through the winter of '62-'63, the Rappahannock marked the boundary line between slavery and freedom.

Many Union soldiers slunk into a deep depression following the battle. They entered what has become known as the "Valley Forge Winter" of the war. Most were happy just to have survived the seemingly senseless slaughter in Fredericksburg and to now be tucked behind the protective barrier of the Rappahannock River. One Pennsylvania soldier perhaps summed up the feelings of the Army of the Potomac best:

I am free to confess that the moment I touched the earth I drew a long, strong and soul-relieving breath, and from the bottom of

my heart, thanked god that I have lived to get out of that infernal slaughter pen and was once more safely landed on the other side of Jordan.

Fredericksburg National Cemetery

Ambrose Burnside had come to Fredericksburg hoping to find an open road to Richmond and a pathway to the victory Lincoln so desperately needed to support the Emancipation Proclamation. Instead, Burnside's army suffered its most lopsided defeat of the war.

He found—as Lee had put it—"war so terrible."

"It is a good thing war is so terrible, or we should grow too fond of it."

— *Robert E. Lee*

107

Christmas on the Rappahannock

POSTSCRIPT

Christmas of 1862 was a bleak holiday for the men of the Army of the Potomac, which sprawled like a huge blue blanket across Stafford County, Virginia, just across the Rappahannock River from the city of Fredericksburg. At least for a short time, the men could look toward Christmas and a short break from the harrowing year that that was wrapping up. The army had stumbled back from the gates of Richmond to the doorstep of Washington; they had lost their beloved commander, George McClellan; and they had been brutally defeated on the outskirts of Fredericksburg.

Observance of the Christmas holiday varied from camp to camp, soldier to soldier. Some, like the men of the 140th Pennsylvania Infantry, found themselves stuck on picket duty along the banks of the river. The unit had been formed in August and September of 1862 and had joined the army in the days following the Fredericksburg defeat. This was their first Christmas away from home.

While on the banks of the Rappahannock, the men started a conversation with the Mississippi troops across the way. After a short while, small boats set sail across the river, and the green Pennsylvanians pulled cords of tobacco from their keep. The boats were refilled with cargo—coffee and newspapers, this time—and were sent back to the south bank of the river. The Christmas spirit was alive and well on the front lines.

In the camps, meanwhile, many of the veteran units suffered from low morale and didn't bother to observe the holiday. Others did what they could to make the best of tough situation. Charles Haydon of the 2nd Michigan wrote of his Christmas feast:

We made Christmas dinner on beef, hard tacks & coffee. I had fortunately completed my meal when Moore made a discovery which checked him midway in his, that the hard tacks were full

109

The modern image of Santa Claus dates back to a sketch by Thomas Nast that appeared on the cover of the January 3, 1863 issue of *Harper's Weekly*. In the image, Santa is visiting a rather dejected Army of the Potomac.

of bugs and worms. This is no uncommon thing of late but his wry face was the most laughable thing of the day.

Soldiers in the 154th New York fared better in their Christmas dining. "[F]or breakfast we had fried pork & fried hard tacks (the hard tacks we have now are not like the ones that we used to get 3 months ago, they are now brittle sweet as any crackers & nearly as tender as soda crackers), Indiana pan cakes & molasses," wrote Emory Sweetland. "For dinner hard tacks & coffee. For supper Indian pudding with sugar out & some tea."

Men serving in the First and Sixth corps were spared from drilling on the holiday. In the camp of the Ninth Corps, Maj. Gen. Edwin Sumner held a grand review of the corps. The camps of the Second Corps busied themselves by constructing log huts for winter quarters. Others in the Second Corps cooked bean soup "…which was very good…" In the Signal Corps, commissaries were issuing, "whiskey to all those applied for it." The next day the Army of the Potomac "was as drunk as an <u>owl</u>…." David Beem of the 14th Indiana claimed that the army was on a "general Christmas drunk."

Those soldiers not on a drunken bender wrote that the Christmas of 1862 was "dull." Letter after letter, diary after diary recorded the word *dull*.

Still, many of the soldiers did what they could to cheer themselves. Letters from home "were welcome Christmas presents." In the days before and after Christmas, packages arrived from home. Newspapers, cakes, dried meats filled the packages. Many soldiers opened the packages with delight and shared the contents with their messmates.

Some of the men turned to music to lift their spirits. On Christmas Eve, men of the 106th Pennsylvania

Soldiers relished letters from home.

> *got up a band; violin, tamporin, banjoe and bones. Also a glee club....So we started out and serenaded several quartermasters, where whe was welcomed and treated with respect. I must say as whe done so well whe at last ventured to serenade our Col and the Col of the first Caliafornia where whe was again welcomed and asked to come in and take some of that what makes people merry on such occasions.*

Those not in the singing and drinking mood adorned camps with boughs of evergreen, which not only brightened the bleak camps with color but also helped to mask the awful smell of the vast campground.

In the end, it was up to each soldier and his pals as to how they would or would not recognize the Christmas holiday. Be it writing letters home, eating, drinking, or doing their best to forget the holiday all together, the men did what they could to cope. Unfortunately for this army, their "Valley Forge Winter" was just getting started. With nearly 135,000 Union soldiers spread across the landscape, Stafford County, Virginia was quickly turning into a barren wasteland. Wood for fires and building cabins was harder and harder to come by, and soldiers had to travel farther to retrieve it. Prospects of the war ending by Christmas 1863 also looked hopeless.

But that all seemed so far ahead. For some of the men, the holiday cheer they found in 1862 was enough: Christmas was a welcome break from war.

Confederates had their share of winter fun, too, including massive snowball battles.

Fredericksburg National Cemetery

APPENDIX A

Fredericksburg National Cemetery, est. in July 1865, is the final resting place for 15,333 American soldiers—15,243 of whom were soldiers of the four major Civil War battles fought in the Fredericksburg area. The balance served in the Spanish-American War, World War I and World War II. The cemetery was closed to new interments in 1945.

No general officers are buried in the cemetery, although the statue of one stands atop a memorial in cemetery's center: Major General Andrew Atkinson Humphreys, whose men assaulted the Sunken Road late in the day on December 13. Humphreys was not killed here, nor does he rest here; his soldiers wanted to memorialize their leader and the heroic valor they had shown at Fredericksburg.

Three other monuments are inside the Fredericksburg National Cemetery. The first is near the cemetery's entrance, dedicated to the Union Fifth Army Corps. A second monument, to the men of the 127th Pennsylvania, sits fifteen yards from the flagpole. The last monument is to a Confederate unit known as Parker's Battery, which fought atop the heights during the Second Battle of Fredericksburg.

No Confederate's were intentionally buried here in the National Cemetery. Those Confederate bodies not brought home by the families have been laid to rest in the Fredericksburg City Cemetery (at the intersection of Washington Ave. and William St.). Just over 3,300 Confederate soldiers are buried there; of those, 2,184 are unknown.

Six Confederate generals are buried in the city cemetery, as is Brigadier General Daniel Davis Wheeler, USA. Wheeler was a staff officer during the Second Battle of Fredericksburg and Salem Church. After the war, he moved to Fredericksburg and married a local woman. For actions at Salem Church, he was awarded the Medal of Honor.

The Jewel on the Rappahannock

APPENDIX B

Located almost directly between Washington, D.C., fifty miles to the north, and Richmond, Virginia, fifty-five miles to the south, Fredericksburg was nearly predestined for doom in the American Civil War.

Fredericksburg, with its wartime population of 5,020, boasted an active port with access to the Chesapeake Bay; a canal; the Richmond, Fredericksburg, & Potomac Railroad; and a series of major roads coming in and out of the city, including the Telegraph Road, which shot like a bullet between Washington and Richmond. All provided avenues for the movement of soldiers and supplies.

Founded in 1727, Fredericksburg was named for Frederick, Prince of Wales and the hated son of King George II. The streets reflected the city's rich colonial history and bore the names of the English-German House of Hanover. William and Hanover streets ran west from the city towards Marye's Heights. Princess Anne, Caroline (the city's main thoroughfare) and other streets ran parallel to the river. At its widest point, the city was barely seven blocks across.

Fredericksburg as seen from Stafford Heights on the far bank.

Many state and national luminaries made their homes in and around the city. George Washington's family owned and operated a ferry crossing at the lower end of the city, and George's mother, Mary Washington, spent the last seventeen years of her life in a home on Charles Street. Washington's sister, Betty, lived in the impressive mansion Kenmore, just a short walk from their mother's. President James Monroe practiced law in the city, as did Virginia governor/Confederate general William "Extra Billy" Smith. Revolutionary war hero John Paul Jones lived in the city, as did patriot-martyr Hugh

The city of Fredericksburg as painted by artist George Frankenstein shortly after the war.

The Rising Sun Tavern is one of several Revolution-era attractions located in the city.

Mercer, who ran an apothecary shop on Caroline Street.

"[Fredericksburg] has long boasted itself as possessing a refined society;" wrote the London *Times,* "which may be interpreted as a society satisfied with the possession of moderate competency, unambitious, devoid of Yankee restlessness and greed."

The small yet thriving business district included thirteen confectioners, two book dealers, and any number of grocers and dry goods dealers. One advertisement described the business of "Hugh Scott, Produce Dealer, Grocer, and Commission Merchant," which "will keep on hand a large stock of Groceries, Guano, Family Flour, Agricultural Implements, &c...." The city also boasted three major churches and several smaller ones, an impressive courthouse, a sash and blind factory, two banks, a market house, and a Masonic Cemetery and Lodge.

"The city of Fredericksburg was an aristocratic and wealthy town," said David Chamberlain of the 4th Michigan. "There was more taste and comfort exhibited in their dwelling than any place I have ever seen south of our Northern cities. The town was lighted with gas and well supplied with good water. The streets and sidewalks in good order, the general location is superb, a valley [of] about two miles wide gradually rising up... until you reach the first range of hills, then running off into a country beautifully rolling."

Not everyone was as impressed with the area. Charley Goddard of the 1st Minnesota described the small village of Falmouth, just across the river, as "one of the most Godforsaken places I ever saw in my life.... The inhabitants that are around

the street standing or leaning up against the corners look as if they had not a friend in the world and if you asked them how they like these visitors, 'Right smart,' will be the answer and you can't get another word out of them."

"The women of this place look as if they could swallow the entire army of live Yankees…" a soldier of the 2nd Wisconsin wrote. "Their 'pouting' and effeminate scowls are amusing to our troops who nearly kill the poor 'secesh creatures' with their Yankee smiles…. Had Barnum's Big Show been in town it would not have attracted half the attention that our distinguished country men did."

The millrace that cut across the open plain to the west of the city, in front of Marye's Heights, emptied back into the Rappahannock at this mill. The railroad bridge that spanned the river was destroyed by Confederates prior to the Union occupation in the spring of '62.

The Federal army that approached the banks of the Rappahannock that spring was not looking to do battle as Burnside's men were the following winter. In reality, the first occupation was quiet, broken only by an occasional bushwhacker raid and the flight of thousands of slaves who freed themselves by crossing into Union lines. After a while, townsfolk even took a shine to the commander of the Union occupiers, Brigadier General John F. Reynolds. Following his stint as the military governor, Reynolds left Fredericksburg and was captured during the Peninsula Campaign. Sent to Libby Prison in Richmond, he was surprised when the citizens of Fredericksburg petitioned his captors to free him.

Princess Anne Street

The U.S. Sanitary Commission set up shop in downtown Fredericksburg during the Union army's occupation of the area in 1864.

Burnside had a much different experience. Most of the city's population packed up and moved away when his army arrived that following December. Over the next few weeks months, the once-impressive city would be ruined by looting, artillery bombardment, and street fighting. For those who came back, it would be like stepping into another universe.

"Almost every house has six or eight shells through it," said one resident; "the doors are wide open, the locks and windows broken, and the shutters torn down. Two blocks of buildings were burned to the ground."

The desolation stuck, too. It would take one hundred years for the city to rebound to its pre-war population.

"Fredericksburg is now a dilapidated place," a member of the United States Sanitary Commission wrote in the summer of '64, when the city was effectively converted into a huge hospital to deal with the wounded men of Ulysses S. Grant's Overland Campaign. "It bears the marks of General Burnside's attack, a year and a half ago. Hardly a house but has been battered by shot or shell. Some entire rows of buildings are in ruins. Apart from the humanity and Christian benevolence we saw exemplified everywhere, it was an awful place. The very buzzards swung themselves lazily over it, attracted by the horrid atmosphere that brooded over it by day and by night."

In St. George's Cemetery on Princess Anne Street, John Paul Jones installed a marker for his deceased brother, William. Although that marker eventually crumbled, admirers of Jones installed a new marker in 1930.

Caught in the Crossfire: Civilians at Fredericksburg

APPENDIX C
BY KATHLEEN LOGOTHETIS

In November 1862, the city of Fredericksburg found itself in the crossfire of the armies of Lee and Burnside. For several months that summer, residents had been forced to deal with the indignities and inconveniences of living in an occupied city. Now the Union army was back once more, and Lee and his army were in place to contest the Federal presence. Fredericksburg, situated between them, braced itself.

"The women of this place look as if they could swallow the entire army of live Yankees..."

Refugees scattered in all directions from the city. Some residents used the railroad to move south to Richmond, Petersburg, or Charlottesville. Many stayed with family members or friends in the country, or sheltered in barns, churches, and outbuildings. Some huddled under tents in makeshift camps, braving the December weather the best they could. One such camp was located on the opposite side of Marye's Heights, behind the Confederate line, and another was located at Salem Church. Several families sought the charity of strangers. Mathilda Hamilton wrote that "[t]he house is as full as it can be, and all our outhouses full. Respectable white people, with their own provisions are refugeeing in our servants houses, and all about in the neighborhood it is the same way."

A week and a half passed before Burnside tried to force his way across the river. Those residents who had stayed in town or who had returned to their homes were caught in the middle of an unexpected artillery bombardment. Hurrying to cellars and basements, families and slaves huddled together as shells tore through their houses. Some families fled, becoming refugees again. Fanny White, with her family and others who sheltered with them, hurried away from their home only partly

dressed, and Jane Beale's family was rescued from their cellar with the help of an ambulance borrowed from the army. A few families were forced out of their homes, such as the eighty-year-old postmaster, Reuben Thom, and his family, who had to escape the flames when shells set their house on fire. At least fifty structures were destroyed by fire during the course of the day. A few civilian lives would be lost, as well, although the details are scarce. Eighteen-year-old Jacob Grotz was apparently killed by an exploding shell, and an African-American woman was also killed by a shell as she huddled under her bed.

Another civilian would become a casualty after the first Union troops had crossed the river and were endeavoring to empty the town of Confederates, moving house by house, street by street. Captain George Macy of the 20th Massachusetts found an old man in one of the houses and placed him in front of his troops as a guide through the streets of Fredericksburg. In the fierce crossfire of the street fight, the guide soon dropped dead, killed by Confederate fire. By nightfall, the Confederates had pulled out of town, and Union soldiers poured over the river on the now-completed bridges. Officers took private residences as their quarters, and soldiers bunked down among the ruins of houses.

December 12 was a day of little fighting between the two armies, giving the Union soldiers time to roam the city of Fredericksburg. Previously, Union armies took great care to protect private property; now they destroyed it at will. "They deserved it all for there is not a stronger secession city in Virginia than Fredericksburg," wrote one soldier and another mused, "[d]o our friends cry out against this? So do we—it is wrong, essentially wrong, but it is War."

Few civilians remained in town during the battle, but for those who did, the sights and sounds of December 13 were as bad as what had come before. Mamie Wells, trapped in her basement with the rest of her family, watched the lines of Union men march past the window towards Marye's Heights:

> *At each charge the roar of musketry—that soul-sickening sound—had the effect of almost stopping my breath. In those moments I pictured to myself the dead and the dying, and wondered why such a cruel thing as war should ever be allowed in a civilized country. That childish wonder still clings to me. We spent that Saturday afternoon huddled together beneath the windows, silently gazing at each other's mournful countenance as we strained our ears to catch every sound, even though they chilled us to the heart.*

As wave after wave of Union attacks failed to take the heights, hundreds of wounded men streamed back into town and sought refuge in any structure they could find. Churches, public buildings, and private homes were all turned into hospitals, and the streets filled with the injured and the dead.

With Burnside's defeat and retreat back across the river, civilians began to emerge from basements and return from their temporary homes to face a town destroyed. Besides the bombed and burned-out buildings, the evidence of looting was overwhelming. "Let us enter this house," wrote Mamie Wells:

> *It belongs to an intelligent, enterprising citizen, who fled with his wife the morning of the eleventh. See the empty portrait frames upon the wall! Upon the floor lies a portion of the canvas, an aged face, mayhap one long since buried beneath the sod. We cannot enter this room; for a barrel of molasses has been poured upon the velvet carpet. The piano is covered with salt pork, the keys are broken and the wires cut. The mirrors are shattered; gas fixtures trampled upon; the bottoms of the sofas are cut out; chairs split with axes, and the plastering, even the laths, torn from the wall. We will go upstairs. Here are the relics of handsome dresses torn to ribbons. There is no bedding—that lies in the street in the mud. This carpet has been spread with butter. The doors of the wardrobes and washstands are broken off, and ruin stamped upon everything around. There is no silver to be found anywhere—a portion of that we have already seen in the possession of a Federal officer. The owner of this*

A battle-damaged home along lower Caroline Street

once pleasant home will return in a few days to find but the shadow of a house; not a change of garments for himself, wife or child; not an article of value left him either at his house or store.

Families took stock of their losses and tried to survive and rebuild. "I can tell you much better what they left," stated Joseph Alsop, "than what they destroyed." Besides the physical damage, injured soldiers remained in town, and dead bodies and fresh graves lay scattered over the landscape. Fredericksburg residents now had to pick up and move on amidst the destruction around them.

The destruction of Fredericksburg shocked the South and fueled anger against the Union troops. Charitable contributions poured in from the Confederacy to help residents survive the winter and rebuild the town. Soldiers in James Longstreet's corps raised $1,391, and in total the city received $170,000 plus gifts of supplies. Even such generosity fell short of the scale of need, and Fredericksburg struggled through the remainder of the war.

December 1862 was not the first time Fredericksburg encountered the armies, and it would not be the last. Situated between the two wartime capitals, the city would play host to both armies several times during the war. The destruction of the city was so bad that some families never returned, and it would take over a century for Fredericksburg to recover. Scars of the ordeal still exist today.

The Ebert House, owned by German immigrants Henry and Sophia Ebert, sat on the corner where the Sunken Road turned away from the base of Marye's Heights toward downtown Fredericksburg. The Eberts ran a small grocery store out of the house. The building survived into the 1950s.

Tour Sites

Aside from the Gordon home along Princess Anne Street where General Howard made his headquarters (as mentioned on pg. 42), several homes that had been the sites of civilian-related stories still stand in downtown Fredericksburg.

Please note that the homes are private residences, so please respect the privacy of the homeowners as you explore the city. Also, exercise caution as you park and get in and out of your vehicle; the city's streets are busy, and the one-way traffic can sometimes be confusing to pedestrians unfamiliar with the traffic patterns.

The former Mamie Wells House on Sophia Street

1. Mamie Wells House *(818 Sophia Street)*

In this house lived "Captain" Wells, his wife, and three daughters. Mamie, the oldest girl, wrote a detailed memoir of her experiences after the war. Hers is the only civilian account of a family who remained in their home for the entire Battle of Fredericksburg. She relates her experiences from the moment the Union army arrived in November, through the bombardment, looting, battle, and aftermath. "To sum up the devastation perpetrated by the Federal troops upon the town of Fredericksburg, during their sojourn there of five nights," she wrote, "I can only say, that unless they had burned every building to the ground, I do not know what more they could have done."

2. Jane Beale House *(307 Lewis Street, at the corner of Charles Street)*

Jane Howison Beale is perhaps Fredericksburg's most famous wartime diarist. A widow with nine children, Jane ran a school in a brick structure next to her house and boarded students for income. She lost a son, Charley, at the Battle of Williamsburg and then endured the bombardment of Fredericksburg in December 1862. Her family's escape by military ambulance is highlighted in the movie *Gods and Generals*. As she fled the city, she saw other refugees behind Marye's Heights: "Crowds of women and children had sought refuge in this sheltered spot and as night drew on they were in great distress…. Some few had stretched blue yarn counterpanes or pieces of old carpet over sticks, stuck in the ground—and the little ones were huddled together under these tents, the women were weeping the children crying loudly, I saw one walking along with a baby in her arms and another little one not three years old clinging to her dress and crying 'I want to go home' My heart ached for them…." Jane's diary abruptly ends after her flight from Fredericksburg and offers us no more clues to her thoughts for the rest of the war.

The former Jane Beale
House on Lewis Street

The former Fannie White
House on Charles Street

3. Fannie White House *(1204 Charles Street)*

Frances White and her three children lived in this home, near
that of Jane Beale and her family. Twelve year old Fannie White
wrote a memoir after the war of her experiences in wartime
Fredericksburg. Like the Beales, the White family endured the
bombardment in their basement, then escaped to safety. They
found refuge at Salem Church, west of town, and returned days
later to a ruined home. In her home "[o]ne room was piled
high, more than half way to the ceiling with feathers from the
beds ripped up. Every mirror was run through with a bayonet,
one panel of each door cut out, altho none of the doors were
locked, and the furniture nearly all broken up."

ONE WAY ←

AUCTION BLOCK
Fredericksburg's
Principal Auction Site
in
Pre-Civil War Days
for
Slaves and Prope
1984
Hi

The Front Line of Emancipation: Slavery at Fredericksburg

APPENDIX D
BY KATHLEEN LOGOTHETIS
& STEWARD HENDERSON

*Think of what it is to be a slave!!! To be treated not as a
man but as a personal chattel, a thing that may be bought
or sold, to have no right to the fruits of your own labour,
no right to your own wife and children…think of this, and
all the nameless horrors that are concentrated in that one
word Slavery.*

The author of this quotation, Fredericksburg resident Mary
Berkeley Minor Blackford, was a member of the American
Colonization Society and kept a journal entitled *Notes Illustrative of the
Wrongs of Slavery*. Influenced by the presence of a slave trader's jail close
to her house and the sight of
slaves driven through the streets,
she was particularly affected
by the request of her cook's
husband to see his wife one last
time after he had been sold.
Because of her commitment
to the cause, she was twice
threatened by the grand jury for
teaching slaves to read the Bible.

Blackford spoke for
a minority in a city where
slavery flourished. Of a total
population in 1860 of 5,026,
there were 3,311 whites, 420 free
blacks, and 1,295 slaves living
in Fredericksburg—an increase

**Blacks—free and enslaved—made up approximately one-third of the
population in Fredericksburg.**

of 120 slaves since the 1850 census. Slaveholders represented
thirty-four percent of the households in town, and there were slave
traders in the area purchasing slaves who would be later sold south.
Fredericksburg was a town filled with such contradictions: most of
its residents and laws were pro-slavery, while a minority supported
colonization and treating blacks more humanely.

Local, state, and federal laws sided with the majority of
Southerners. Local laws stated that slaves must carry passes to
move through town, must clear the sidewalks when a white person

Slave children wash a wagon near the Scott House.

approached, and could not meet among themselves; the penalty for offenses was thirty-nine lashes. State laws penalized any black person who concocted a medicine intended to cause an abortion (slave babies were valuable assets to slaveowners), mandated that freed blacks had to leave Virginia within one year or they would be sold back into slavery, and prohibited free blacks from acquiring slaves (many free blacks owned their family members so that they would not have to leave Virginia). Crimes like burglary and theft held sentences of whipping or execution. At the federal level, the Fugitive Slave Law of 1850 mandated Northerners to help with the capture of fugitive slaves.

The legal system supported the institution of slavery, and so did ideology and misconception. Whites said that if blacks were emancipated, black men would marry white women, a mixing of the races called miscegenation. Ironically, miscegenation was primarily instigated by the white male slaveowners, their male offspring, and overseers who had children with slave women.

Many Southerners believed that slaves were happy because of their singing and smiling faces. In reality, slaves knew that if they smiled they were less likely to be beaten. Their singing held several messages – including freedom and the pace of working in the fields.

Not all slaveowners were cruel. In Fredericksburg, many of the slaveowners treated their slaves well, and several slaves stayed with their former masters well after the Civil War was over. However, slave-owners always held the power of family separation over their slaves—a fact always more important to most slaves than freedom or punishment.

However, slavery was changing in Fredericksburg from rural to urban slavery. Rural slavery, the most common type,

As many as ten thousand slaves fled to freedom when the Union Army occupied the region.

pertained to plantations and farms where slaves were house servants or field hands. Urban slavery was the hiring out of slaves to perform skilled and unskilled labor in towns and cities. For example, hired slaves could work in stores, hotels, and bars, in tobacco factories, or as blacksmiths. These slaves could earn wages if they worked over the time for which they were hired, and they had a lot more freedom. Many learned to read and write, mingled more freely with free blacks, and learned about current events.

Fredericksburg slave John Washington wrote about being hired out in Richmond and Fredericksburg. John's mother was a mulatto slave, and his father was a white man, so he looked white. When the Union army approached Fredericksburg in April 1862, he worked in the Shakespeare Hotel as the bartender. When all the white men evacuated the town, he was given money to pay all of the hired help. He did, then poured them all a drink and told them the Yankees were coming. He eventually talked with Union soldiers and crossed the Rappahannock River to freedom. Mistaken as a white man, Washington informed the Federals he'd been a slave all his life. But "with the help of God," he later said, "I never would be a Slave no more." Washington hired himself as a mess servant and a scout for the Union army and was even taken into Fredericksburg to identify the prominent Rebels in the town, who were promptly arrested.

John Washington was one of over 10,000 slaves who escaped Fredericksburg and the surrounding areas during the Union army's occupation. Many of the slaveowners were unhappy and surprised that their "servants" left them, but if Washington's tale is any indication, the newly freed blacks looked only forward: "I began now to feel that life had a new Joy awaiting me."

John Washington

Fredericksburg in Memory

APPENDIX E

BY CHRIS MACKOWSKI

One of the most-repeated misconceptions about Fredericksburg goes something like this: The Union army, trapped on the north side of the Rappahannock River, waiting in vain for pontoon boats to arrive, could have easily waded across the river just north of Fredericksburg. Instead, army commander Maj. Gen. Ambrose Burnside frittered away his element of surprise. The delay cost him weeks, ultimately leading to the foolish and vain headlong assaults against the Sunken Road and Stone Wall.

Popular literature has helped solidify the myth in public consciousness. According to such accounts, Union division commander Brig. Gen. Winfield Scott Hancock, frustrated by the endless wait for the pontoons, walks down to the riverbank on a frosty morning and, there, happens to see a herd of cows cross the Rappahannock. When he points this out to the high command and pleads his case for wading across, he's rebuffed by a blustery commander who knows better than the meddling subordinate. Hancock personifies the frustration of the Union army and the desire of the men to get across and strike a blow.

Above the fall line, the Rappahannock River is shallow enough to walk across, and it has a rocky riverbottom.

Because Burnside is already so easy to vilify, most people accept the anecdote as further proof that he was inept. The misconceptions captured in this episode add fuel to the fire that has scorched his reputation.

So, why *didn't* the army just walk across?

After all, the Rappahannock *is* shallow enough to wade across just north of town. The river, flowing east, makes a wide bend southward, descending a series of rocky falls before smoothing out just as it flows past by town. There, below the fall line, the Rappahannock gets deeper and wider, and it rises and falls with the tug of the far-off tide.

It's there, directly opposite the town, across the deeper, wider section of river, that Burnside built his pontoon bridges when they finally arrived.

An annual Memorial Day commemoration in the national cemetery draws thousands of visitors.

To understand Burnside's decision to stay put and not wade, it's important to challenge the assumptions one makes about river crossings. There is a difference between 'a crossing of a river' and 'a *military* crossing of a river. It's one thing to deploy infantry across a ford, but the infantry can't advance far with out the support of the artillery and the wagon train.

The rocky stretch of river Hancock pointed out would not have been wheel-friendly, so wagons would have had a tough time crossing. To position part of the army across the river in hostile territory with only the supplies they could carry—that would be a precarious choice.

The same would have been true for artillery trying to cross over the craggy-bottomed river. Cannons, like wagons, depended on a wheel-friendly crossing, meaning the artillery would have had a tougher time getting across the river than the cows Hancock allegedly spotted. (As it happened, once the army did cross for battle, the deployment of its artillery on the northern end of the field was almost completely ineffectual.)

Burnside had reason to be concerned about the river. He didn't have the benefit of the Weather Channel to tell him what might be blowing in from the west, nor could he tell what the weather was like out near the river's headwaters. A rainstorm could make water levels rise precipitously, and if that happened with part of the army on the far bank, those men would be cut off, making them vulnerable. Consider how much more vulnerable they would have been, too, without ready supplies or artillery support.

Burnside must certainly shoulder the responsibility for the way he handled the army during the Fredericksburg campaign, but it's wrong to automatically assume every decision he made was an incompetent one.

Misconceptions about the river crossing are typical of the ways in which people have historically misunderstood the battle of Fredericksburg. Such misconceptions are often based on poorly understood assumptions that get passed down from one generation to the next or that get perpetuated in popular culture.

Another example would be the attention historians and buffs alike have given the attacks against the Stone Wall while virtually ignoring the attacks at the south end of the field against Prospect Hill. The placement of the Visitor Center near the Sunken Road and the Civilian Conservation Corps' work to restore the Stone Wall both ensured that part of the story would get the most focus because visitors would stop there by default.

At that time—in the 1930s—historians understood the battle differently than they did today. In fact, only in the 1990s did the story begin to shift when National Park Service Historian Frank O'Reilly uncovered new information. Burnside and Left Grand Division commander William B. Franklin were working from mismatched maps, which (in part) explains Burnside's apparently confusing orders. Burnside's muddy writing made the problem worse, and Franklin's inexplicable failure to ask for clarification proved to be the disastrous last straw. Once O'Reilly pieced that misunderstood puzzle together, the entire focus of the battle shifted

Construction of the Fredericksburg Battlefield Visitor Center (right) and carriage house (left), which now serves as the park's bookstore.

southward: Burnside planned to launch his main attack against Prospect Hill, not the Stone Wall.

So how did the Stone Wall, then, become the focal point of attention? First, numbers alone tell how tragic the story there is: close to 8,000 Union casualties versus fewer than 1,000 Confederate casualties. Then, consider the futility of the scenario: Union soldiers had to charge uphill across open ground that was slippery with mud, storming a strongly fortified Confederate position dominated by imposing artillery. To the modern eye, it looks like a ready-made disaster, so it's hard to wonder how Burnside couldn't have seen it.

In fact, Burnside did. But the attacks against the Stone Wall were meant only as a diversion to prevent Confederate reinforcements from shifting south. The attacks took on an awful life of their own, though—in part, as a way to keep up pressure so that Confederates wouldn't storm over the wall and counterattack.

After the war, Union veterans did much to perpetuate the story of the attacks against Marye's Heights because it was there that the Union army truly did prove its mettle. Much has been glorified about the Southern fighting élan, but at Fredericksburg, Union soldiers proved they were every bit as tough and determined as Confederates. Veterans did much to remind subsequent generations of that.

The Irish, in particular, had much to gain. As an ethnic group in the mid-nineteenth century, the Irish were at the bottom of the social ladder, and they faced heavy discrimination. The charge of the Irish Brigade, especially coming on the heels of their charge against the Sunken Road at Antietam, demonstrated Irish courage and worth—and Irishmen everywhere pushed the story with zeal as a way of reinforcing their own sense of American identity and patriotism. As historian Craig A. Warren has written, several veterans of the brigade were particularly influential in

The Park Service's early interpretation along Lee Drive reflects the strong negative bias against Confederate Lt. Gen. James Longstreet prevalent across the South for so long—a bias that makes up a key tenet of Lost Cause mythology. On Longstreet's sector of the field, the First Corps commander was infrequently mentioned in favor of his division commanders (such as Hood, above); on Jackson's sector, however, the Second Corps commander was named while his division commanders went unmentioned.

pushing the story through their postwar writings. "Refusing to let history dismiss as meaningless the Irish blood spilled at Fredericksburg, these men forged a body of literature remarkable for its propensity to mythologize Irish participation in the Civil War," he writes. A lot of brave men charged the wall that day, but the Irish are the ones most frequently remembered because they made a concerted effort to make sure they'd be remembered.

Pop culture has continued to perpetuate that memory. One of the longest—and, frankly, most tangential—scenes in the movie *Gods and Generals* focuses on the charge of the Irish Brigade. Civil War paintings depicting the charge remain popular. Even the Park Service, as part of anniversary commemorations, includes a march in the Brigade's footsteps.

On the Confederate side, Lost Cause interpretation drove much of the remembrance. Park Service historians, while developing the park's initial interpretation consulted with noted pro-Southern historians like Douglas Southall Freeman. "The Park Service's reliance upon these outside reviewers, each with their veneration for the Confederate cause, ensured that national park exhibits stayed away from controversial topics such as slavery and the causes of the war," a park history noted in 2011.

As a result, Lt. Gen. James Longstreet, whose men held the Sunken Road and Marye's Heights, gets little credit for the Confederate defense during the battle because of his postwar criticisms of Lee and his fallout with the most ardent of the Lost Cause writers like Jubal Early, Fitzhugh Lee, and Daniel Harvey Hill. Lt. Gen. Stonewall Jackson, on the other hand, who left a gap in his lines that Federals charged into, became the great Martyr of the Lost Cause and so is memorialized with his own monument marking his place on the field. Signs along Lee Drive further reflect the bias by marking the location of "Jackson's Corps" while ignoring Longstreet in favor of his division commanders.

Pro-Southern historians like Douglas Southall Freeman (here speaking at an event at Chancellorsville in the 1930s) had a major influence on the park's earliest interpretation, affecting for decades the way the public has understood—and misunderstood—the battle of Fredericksburg.

The battle of Fredericksburg represented the nadir of Union forces in the east, and so it was not an experience most soldiers wanted to remember, which explains why so much of the Union position has been lost to development over time. No one wanted to invest much effort to preserve a memory so painful. As a result, Confederate memory reigned supreme over the battlefield as a lasting testament to their victory there in battle. We remember the story today largely on those terms—which is why it's so easy to dismiss Burnside as a buffoon. That's the way history—not necessarily his own actions—has cast him.

"Whatever Happened To...?"

Major General Ambrose Everett Burnside

Burnside was the shortest-tenured commander of the Army of the Potomac. In January 1863, he led the army on a failed march around Lee's left flank—known today as "The Mud March." Following his removal from command, he was reinstated to command his old Ninth Army Corps, and together they were shipped west to the Department of Ohio. In the fall of 1863, he successfully defended the city of Knoxville, Tennessee from siege by Confederate forces led by Lt. Gen. James Longstreet.

In the spring of 1864, Burnside and his corps were reattached to the Army of the Potomac, but their below-average performance left army commander Lt. Gen. Ulysses S. Grant underwhelmed. Burnside's mediocrity eventually led to the debacle known as the Battle of the Crater in July of 1864 outside Petersburg, which Grant called "the saddest affair I have witnessed in the war." Burnside was removed from field command in August.

Though a failure prior to and during the war, Burnside excelled in the postwar years. He served as the first president of the National Rifle Association, managed several railroads, was three times elected to the governorship of Rhode Island. Rhode Islanders later elected him to the United States Senate.

Burnside died on September 13, 1881. He's buried in Swan Point Cemetery in Providence, Rhode Island.

Major General William Buell Franklin

Franklin holds much of the blame for the failure on the south end of the Fredericksburg battlefield. In an effort to dodge blame, he and a number of his officers undermined Burnside's authority the weeks following the battle. The efforts backfired, though: following Burnside's removal from command in January, Franklin, too, was ousted. He later found himself in the backwater of the war, commanding the Nineteenth Corps in the Army of the Gulf during the ill-fated Red River Campaign, where he was wounded. At the end of the war, Franklin resigned his commission with the army.

Following the war, Franklin served as the general manager of the Colt Fire Arms Manufacturing Company for twenty-two years. He also oversaw the construction of the Connecticut capitol and served as the commissioner general of the Paris Exposition. He died on March 8, 1903.

Major General Joseph Hooker

"Fighting Joe" Hooker was a star on the rise in the Army of the Potomac. He is the only Grand Division commander to stay with the army following the winter shakeup; in fact, he received command of the army from President Lincoln in January 1863—to the chagrin of many officers. He proved to be a more-than-capable organizer and administrator, though, and he quickly restored the confidence that the army had left behind at Marye's Heights.

In April of 1863, Hooker led the army around Lee's right flank and engaged the Army of Northern Virginia at the Battle of Chancellorsville, twelve miles west of Fredericksburg. However, Lee and Jackson got the better of Hooker, who was wounded in the battle. In the post-battle fallout, Hooker engaged in a power struggle with General-in-Chief Halleck. The struggle came to a head in the days prior to Gettysburg, and Hooker was relieved of command. Meade took his place.

For a time, no one knew what to do with Hooker. In the fall of 1863, two corps from the Army of the Potomac were shipped to the Western Theater, and Hooker was sent with them as their commander. Merged into a single corps known as the Twentieth Corps Army of the Cumberland, they performed well under Hooker's leadership until July 1864 when Hooker was passed over for promotion in favor of an incompetent, but less politically inclined, subordinate. Hooker asked to be relieved. Relegated to backwater commands, "Fighting Joe" saw no more fighting.

In 1868, the former general suffered a stroke, which partially paralyzed him for the rest of his life. He died on October 31, 1879.

Major General George Gordon Meade

Meade's star was on the rise following Fredericksburg. Following the battle, he was promoted to command the Fifth Army Corps. Although the position was rightfully his, the man

he succeeded, Brigadier General Daniel Butterfield, held a lifelong grudge against him for it.

In June 1863, just three days before the battle of Gettysburg, Meade was promoted to command the entire army of the Potomac. The Pennsylvanian would eventually serve as the army's longest-tenured commander, holding the position from Gettysburg until after Lee's capitulation at Appomattox Court House.

Meade's efforts were greatly overshadowed by Lt. Gen. Ulysses S. Grant, who attached himself to Meade's headquarters in April 1864 after Grant was promoted to command all Union armies. Although Grant took an increasingly active role in the management of the Army of the Potomac, he recommended Meade for further promotion. "Meade has more than met my most sanguine expectations. He and [William T.] Sherman are the fittest officers for large commands I have come in contact with," Grant said.

Following the war, Meade held various posts in the peacetime army. He died on November 6, 1872 of pneumonia. He is buried in Philadelphia's Laurel Hill Cemetery.

After his death death, Meade's family endured numerous attacks on Meade's character from the unsavory elements of the former Army of the Potomac, including attacks led by Butterfield and another rival, Maj. Gen. Dan Sickles, who embroiled himself in controversy with Meade after Sickles disobeyed orders during the battle of Gettysburg.

Brigadier General Thomas Francis Meagher

The Irish Nationalist was a mixed bag as battlefield leader. His famed brigade was decimated at Antietam and Marye's Heights. A shell of its former self after that, the brigade saw little action at Chancellorsville, so Meagher requested to return to New York to recruit and replenish the brigade's depleted ranks. He was denied the request and attempted to resign his commission in the army. At first he was able to resign, but later the order was rescinded. Instead, he was placed in command of a provisional division in William T. Sherman's western army in 1864. He finally retired from the army in May 1865.

Later, Meagher served as territorial secretary and governor of Montana. In 1867, while on a riverboat, Meagher fell into the Missouri River and drowned. While it was reported that Meagher was drunk when he fell overboard, some conspiracy theorists speculated that Meagher was murdered by agents of the British Government, who wanted rid of the Irish instigator once and for all.

Major General Edwin Voss Sumner

Sumner was the oldest Union general to serve at the battle of Fredericksburg and the oldest corps commander to serve on either side in the war. Sumner's position with the army was safe following the battle, but when Lincoln relieved Burnside from command and replaced him with Maj. Gen. Joseph Hooker, Sumner—who detested Hooker—asked to be relieved of command. He was assigned to the Department of Missouri, but died on March 21, 1863 at his daughter's home in Syracuse, New York, before he was able to join his new command.

General Robert Edward Lee

Robert E. Lee is arguably the most famous general to come out of the American Civil War.

Following the battle of Fredericksburg, Lee's army went into winter encampment in late January 1863. In April, he and his third-in-command, Thomas J. "Stonewall" Jackson, engaged and defeated the Army of the Potomac at Chancellorsville. To maintain the momentum, Lee then led his army north into Pennsylvania, but they met defeat in July at Gettysburg. In the days following the battle, the Army of Northern Virginia slunk back into friendly territory. The war would never be the same again.

Lee did what he could to keep his army in fighting shape, but dwindling supplies and manpower stressed the army. Then, in the spring of 1864, a new adversary entered the Eastern Theater: Lt. Gen. Ulysses S. Grant. Grant battered Lee's outmanned army at every turn, beginning in early May in the Wilderness and continuing through battle or maneuver all the way until mid-June, when the opponents settled into a siege around Petersburg. Lee and his army were, for all intents and purposes, out of the war as a fighting unit, although the siege would last until Grant finally broke Lee's line in April of 1864. Grant finally chased Lee down at Appomattox Court House, where "the Old Gray Fox" surrendered his army.

Following the war, the famed Virginian embraced peace and accepted the presidency of Washington College in Lexington Virginia (today's Washington and Lee University). While in Lexington, Lee gathered papers to write a memoir on his participation in the war. Unfortunately, his book never saw the light of day. On Sept. 28, 1870, he suffered a stroke, and his condition steadily deteriorated. He finally died on October 12, 1870, just five years after he surrendered his famed army at Appomattox. He is buried in a family tomb beneath the college chapel at Washington and Lee.

Lieutenant General James Longstreet

During the long hard winter of 1862-63, Lee sent Longstreet and two of his divisions to southeastern Virginia to obtain supplies for the army and besiege the Union-held city of Suffolk. Longstreet failed to break the Union hold on the area, while at the same time missing the Battle of Chancellorsville. During a stop in Richmond on his way back north, he participate in Stonewall Jackson's funeral procession through the streets of the capital.

At Gettysburg, Longstreet's men fought valiantly but failed to secure their objectives. After the army's retreat into Virginia, Longstreet pushed hard to be shipped west with his corps to fight on other fields. His men performed well at Chickamauga, but during the siege of Chattanooga, he made a nuisance of himself to his commander, Maj. Gen. Braxton Bragg.

During the winter of 1863-64, Longstreet operated independently in Tennessee. He besieged Ambrose Burnside and his men at Knoxville but failed to dislodge the former Army of the Potomac commander.

In the spring, Longstreet was recalled to the Eastern Theater and rejoined Lee on the second day of the Battle of the Wilderness, arriving at the right place, at the right time, saving the Army of Northern Virginia. Later in the day, Longstreet launched a successful flank attack, but like Stonewall Jackson was shot accidentally by his own men in the confusion. Longstreet survived the ugly wound to his right shoulder and throat, but did not return to the army until October 1864. By then, the army was being strangled in siege around Petersburg.

Longstreet is Lee's only senior subordinate at Fredericksburg to survive the war. He surrendered with Lee's army, but in the postwar years earned a reputation as a "scalawag" to many Confederate veterans because he became both a Catholic and Republican, and he supported Ulysses S. Grant's presidential campaign. As a reward, Grant appointed him surveyor of customs in New Orleans; later, President Rutherford B. Hayes appointed him U.S. Minister to Turkey. Longstreet also served as a U.S. commissioner of railroads in the late 1890s.

A headstrong man, Longstreet made the mistake of being an outspoken critic of the way Lee handled the army, earning him the eternal ire of Lost Cause revisionists ever since.

Lee's former second-in-command died on January 2, 1904, six days before his 83rd birthday. He is buried in Alta Vista Cemetery in Gainseville, Georgia.

Lieutenant General Thomas Jonathan "Stonewall" Jackson

Lee's third-in-command stayed in the Fredericksburg area through the winter. In April of 1863, his wife Mary Anna arrived just south of the city with their infant daughter, Julia. It was the first time the father had met his child. Over the next few days, the hardened general fawned over her, revealing a side of himself his staff and soldiers had never seen. The Jacksons had Julia baptized by his friend and chaplain, Beverly Tucker Lacy. The general sat for a picture in the Thomas Yerby House of Belvoir—the last picture taken of the man.

When Hooker's army began to move in late April, Mary Anna and Julia were whisked away to Richmond while Jackson turned west to meet the foe. He launched one of the most daring assaults on the war on May 2, 1863, marching around the unprotected right flank of Hooker's army, catching the Federals by surprise. While at the height of his success, though, Jackson rode between the battle lines in the dark to scout the Federal position. As he was returning to his lines, his own men accidentally shot him. Although his left arm had to be amputated as a result, the wounds were not fatal.

Jackson was transported to Guinea Station, Virginia, where doctors expected to evacuate him to Richmond where he could convalesce in peace and quiet. They expected a full recovery. By the time he arrived there, however, a Union cavalry raid had destroyed the tracks. As they waited for repairs, Jackson stayed in a small office building on the Chandler plantation; by the time the repairs were made, Jackson's condition had unexpectedly deteriorated because of pneumonia. The illness claimed his life on Sunday, May 10, 1863. He was laid to rest in Lexington's City Cemetery.

Major General James Ewell Brown "Jeb" Stuart

Lee's bold cavalier performed well at Fredericksburg—a performance he repeated at Chancellorsville, where he and his cavalry gained invaluable intelligence for Jackson and Lee. Following Jackson's wounding, Stuart assumed command of Jackson's corps.

Following Chancellorsville, Stuart reverted back to cavalry command. In June 1863, he was caught off guard and taken to the ropes by Federal cavalry at Brandy Station. To win back his honor, he proposed a ride around the Union army, but he unexpectedly found himself trapped in the process, separated from Lee's army even as it moved north into Pennsylvania. As

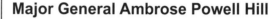

a result, Stuart (and Longstreet) would unrightfully receive the bulk of the blame for the Confederate loss at Gettysburg.

By early 1864, Stuart and his cavalry were back in their old fighting form. In the opening days of Grant's Overland Campaign, Stuart's men parried every thrust from Grant and Meade's cavalry. However, on May 11, 1864, Stuart was mortally wounded in the Battle of Yellow Tavern, outside of Richmond. He died the next day. He is buried in Richmond's Hollywood Cemetery.

Major General Ambrose Powell Hill

Jackson's second-in-command was stuck with his rival until May 2, 1863, when he and Jackson were both wounded at part of the flank attack. A shell fragment clipped Hill in the heel minutes after Jackson had been shot. Following the battle and Jackson's death, Hill was assigned to command the newly organized Third Army Corps.

Little Powell was the best division commander in the Army of Northern Virginia, but as a corps commander, he lacked the dash and élan he had shown while at the head of the Light Division. Hill's lackluster performance at Gettysburg and near-disastrous performance at Bristoe Station showed that he had risen to a level of command beyond his abilities.

In the spring of 1864, Hill was racked by illness and so was in and out of command during the Overland Campaign. He stayed with the army until the end of the Siege of Petersburg, though. On April 2, 1865, as the Confederate line collapsed, Hill was killed by Pennsylvania troops as he was making his way back to his headquarters. He is buried in Richmond's Hollywood Cemetery.

Order of Battle
BATTLE OF FREDERICKSBURG

THE ARMY OF THE POTOMAC
Maj. Gen. Ambrose E. Burnside

ESCORT, ETC...
Oneida (New York) Cavalry · 1st U. S. Cavalry (detachment)
4th U.S. Cavalry, Companies A and E

PROVOST GUARD
Brig. Gen. Marsena R. Patrick
McClellan (Illinois) Dragoons, Company A · McClellan (Illinois)
Dragoons, Company B · 9th New York Infantry, Company G
93d New York Infantry · 2d U.S. Cavalry · 8th U. S. Infantry

VOLUNTEER ENGINEER BRIGADE
Brig. Gen. Daniel P. Woodbury
15th New York · 50th New York · Battalion United States Engineers

ARTILLERY
Brig. Gen. Henry J. Hunt
Artillery Reserve Lieut. Col. William Hays
New York Light, 5th Battery · 1st Battalion New York Light,
Battery A · 1st Battalion New York Light, Battery B
1st Battalion New York Light, Battery C · 1st Battalion New York Light,
Battery D · 1st United States, Battery K · 2d United States, Battery A
4th United States, Battery G · 5th United States, Battery K
32d Massachusetts Infantry, Company C

Unattached Artillery Maj. Thomas S. Trumbull
1st Connecticut Heavy, Battery B · 1st Connecticut Heavy, Battery M

RIGHT GRAND DIVISION Maj. Gen. Edwin V. Sumner

SECOND ARMY CORPS Maj. Gen. Darius N. Couch
First Division Brig. Gen. Winfield S. Hancock
First Brigade Brig. Gen. John C. Caldwell;
Col. George W. Von Schack
5th New Hampshire · 7th New York · 61st New York
64th New York · 81st Pennsylvania · 145th Pennsylvania

Second Brigade Brig. Gen. Thomas F. Meagher
28th Massachusetts · 63d New York · 69th New York
88th New York · 116th Pennsylvania

Third Brigade Col. Samuel K Zook
27th Connecticut · 2d Delaware · 52d New York
57th New York · 66th New York · 53d Pennsylvania

Artillery
1st New York Light, Battery B · 4th United States, Battery C

Second Division Brig. Gen. Oliver O. Howard
First Brigade Brig. Gen. Alfred Sully
19th Maine · 15th Massachusetts · Massachusetts Sharpshooters,
1st Company · 1st Minnesota · Minnesota Sharpshooters,
2d Company · 34th New York · 82d New York (2d Militia)

Second Brigade Col. Joshua T. Owen
69th Pennsylvania · 71st Pennsylvania · 72d Pennsylvania
106th Pennsylvania

Third Brigade Col. Norman J. Hall; Col. William R. Lee
19th Massachusetts · 20th Massachusetts · 7th Michigan
42d New York · 59th New York · 127th Pennsylvania

Artillery
1st Rhode Island Light, Battery A · 1st Rhode Island Light, Battery B

Third Division Brig. Gen. William H. French
First Brigade Brig. Gen. Nathan Kimball;
Col. John S. Mason
14th Indiana · 24th New Jersey · 28th New Jersey · 4th Ohio
8th Ohio · 7th West Virginia

Second Brigade Col. Oliver H. Palmer
14th Connecticut · 108th New York · 130th Pennsylvania

Third Brigade Col. John W. Andrews;
Lieut. Col. William Jameson; Lieut. Col. John W. Marshall
1st Delaware · 4th New York · 10th New York · 132d Pennsylvania

Artillery
1st New York Light, Battery G · 1st Rhode Island Light, Battery G

ARTILLERY RESERVE Capt. Charles Morgan
1st United States, Battery I · 4th United States, Battery A

NINTH ARMY CORPS Brig. Gen. Orlando B. Willcox
ESCORT
6th New York Cavalry, Company B · 6th New York Cavalry, Company C

First Division Brig. Gen. William W. Burns
First Brigade Col. Orlando M. Poe
2d Michigan · 17th Michigan · 20th Michigan · 79th New York

Second Brigade Col. Benjamin C. Christ
29th Massachusetts · 8th Michigan · 27th New Jersey
46th New York · 50th Pennsylvania

Third Brigade Col. Daniel Leasure
36th Massachusetts · 45th Pennsylvania · 100th Pennsylvania

Artillery
1st New York Light, Battery D · 3d United States, Batteries L and M

Second Division Brig. Gen. Samuel D. Sturgis
First Brigade Brig. Gen. James Nagle
2d Maryland · 6th New Hampshire · 9th New Hampshire
48th Pennsylvania · 7th Rhode Island · 12th Rhode Island

Second Brigade Brig. Gen. Edward Ferrero
21st Massachusetts · 35th Massachusetts · 11th New Hampshire
51st New York · 51st Pennsylvania

Artillery
2d New York Light, Battery L · Pennsylvania Light, Battery D
1st Rhode Island Light, Battery D · 4th United States, Battery E

Third Division Brig. Gen. George W. Getty
First Brigade Col. Rush C. Hawkins
10th New Hampshire · 13th New Hampshire · 25th New Jersey
9th New York · 89th New York · 103d New York

Second Brigade Col. Edward Harland
8th Connecticut · 11th Connecticut · 15th Connecticut
16th Connecticut · 4th Rhode Island

Artillery
2d United States, Battery E · 5th United States, Battery A

Cavalry Division Brig. Gen. Alfred Pleasonton
First Brigade Brig. Gen. John F. Farnsworth
8th Illinois · 3d Indiana · 8th New York

Second Brigade Col. David McM. Gregg;
Col. Thomas C. Devin
6th New York · 8th Pennsylvania · 6th United States

Artillery
2d United States, Battery M

CENTER GRAND DIVISION Maj. Gen. Joseph Hooker

THIRD ARMY CORPS Brig. Gen. George Stoneman
First Division Brig. Gen. David B. Birney
First Brigade Brig. Gen. John C. Robinson
20th Indiana · 63d Pennsylvania · 68th Pennsylvania
105th Pennsylvania · 114th Pennsylvania · 141st Pennsylvania

147

Second Brigade Brig. Gen. J. H. Hobart Ward
3d Maine · 4th Maine · 38th New York · 40th New York
55th New York · 57th Pennsylvania · 99th Pennsylvania

Third Brigade Brig. Gen. Hiram G. Berry
17th Maine · 3d Michigan · 5th Michigan · 1st New York
37th New York · 101st New York

Artillery Capt. George Randolph
1st Rhode Island Light, Battery E · 3d United States Batteries F and K

Second Division Brig. Gen. Daniel E. Sickles
First Brigade Brig. Gen. Joseph B. Carr
1st Massachusetts · 11th Massachusetts · 16th Massachusetts
2d New Hampshire · 11th New Jersey · 26th Pennsylvania

Second Brigade Col. George B. Hall
70th New York · 71st New York · 72d New York · 73d New York
74th New York · 120th New York

Third Brigade Brig. Gen. Joseph W. Revere
5th New Jersey · 6th New Jersey · 7th New Jersey · 8th New Jersey
2d New York · 115th Pennsylvania

Artillery Capt. James E. Smith
New Jersey Light, 2d Battery · New York Light, 4th Battery
1st United States, Battery H · 4th United States, Battery K

Third Division Brig. Gen. Amiel W. Whipple
First Brigade Brig. Gen. A. Sanders Piatt;
Col. Emlen Franklin
86th New York · 124th New York · 122d Pennsylvania

Second Brigade Col. Samuel S. Carroll
12th New Hampshire · 163d New York · 84th Pennsylvania
110th Pennsylvania

Artillery
New York Light, 10th Battery · New York Light, 11th Battery
1st Ohio Light. Battery H

FIFTH ARMY CORPS Brig. Gen. Daniel Butterfield
First Division Brig. Gen. Charles Griffin
First Brigade Col. James Barnes
2d Maine · Massachusetts Sharpshooters, 2d Company
18th Massachusetts · 22d Massachusetts · 1st Michigan
13th New York · 25th New York · 118th Pennsylvania

Second Brigade Col. Jacob B. Swkitzer
9th Massachusetts · 32d Massachusetts · 4th Michigan
14th New York · 62d Pennsylvania

Third Brigade Col. T. B. W. Stockton
20th Maine · Michigan Sharpshooters, Brady's Company
16th Michigan · 12th New York · 17th New York
44th New York · 83d Pennsylvania

Artillery
Massachusetts Light, 3d Battery (C) · Massachusetts Light, 5th Battery (E)
1st Rhode Island-Light, Battery C · 5th United States, Battery D

Sharpshooters
1st United States

Second Division Brig. Gen. George Sykes
First Brigade Lieut. Col. Robert C. Buchanan
3d United States · 4th United States · 12th United States
12th United States, 2d Battalion · 14th United States, 1st Battalion
14th United States, 2d Battalion

Second Brigade Maj. George L. Andrews;
Maj. Charles S. Lovell
1st and 2d United States (battalion) · 6th United States
7th United States (battalion) · 10th United States
11th United States · 17th and 19th United States (battalion)

Third Brigade Brig. Gen. Gouverneur K. Warren
5th New York · 140th New York · 146th New York

Artillery
1st Ohio Light, Battery L · 5th United States, Battery I

Third Division Brig. Gen. Andrew A. Humphreys
First Brigade Brig. Gen. Erastus B. Tyler
91st Pennsylvania · 126th Pennsylvania · 129th Pennsylvania
134th Pennsylvania

Second Brigade Col. Peter H. Allabach
123d Pennsylvania · 131st Pennsylvania · 133d Pennsylvania
155th Pennsylvania

Artillery
1st New York Light, Battery C · 1st United States, Batteries E and G

CAVALRY BRIGADE Brig. Gen. William W. Averell
1st Massachusetts · 3d Pennsylvania · 4th Pennsylvania
5th United States

Artillery
2d United States, Batteries B and L

LEFT GRAND DIVISION Maj. Gen. William B. Franklin
ESCORT 6th Pennsylvania Cavalry

FIRST ARMY CORPS Maj. Gen. John F. Reynolds
ESCORT 1st Maine Cavalry, Company L
First Division Brig. Gen. Abner Doubleday
First Brigade Col. Walter Phelps, Jr.
22d New York · 24th New York · 30th New York
84th New York (14th Militia) · 2d U. S. Sharpshooters

Second Brigade Col. James Gavin
7th Indiana · 76th New York · 95th New York · 56th Pennsylvania

Third Brigade Col. William F. Rogers
21st New York · 23d New York · 35th New York
80th New York (20th Militia)

Fourth Brigade Brig. Gen. Solomon Meredith;
Col. Lysander Cutler
19th Indiana · 24th Michigan · 2d Wisconsin · 6th Wisconsin
7th Wisconsin

Artillery Capt. George A. Gerrish; Capt. John A. Reynolds
New Hampshire Light, 1st Battery · 1st New York Light, Battery L
4th United States, Battery B

Second Division Brig. Gen. John Gibbon;
Brig. Gen. Nelson Taylor
First Brigade Col. Adrian R. Root
16th Maine · 94th New York · 104th New York · 105th New York
107th Pennsylvania

Second Brigade Col. Peter Lyle
12th Massachusetts · 26th New York · 90th Pennsylvania
136th Pennsylvania

Third Brigade Brig. Gen. Nelson Taylor;
Col. Samuel H. Leonard
13th Massachusetts · 83d New York (9th Militia)
97th New York · 11th Pennsylvania · 88th Pennsylvania

Artillery Capt. George F. Leppien
Maine Light, 2d Battery · Maine Light, 5th Battery
Pennsylvania Light, Battery C · 1st Pennsylvania Light, Battery F

Third Division Maj. Gen. George G. Meade
First Brigade Col. William Sinclair;
Col. William McCandless
1st Pennsylvania Reserves · 2d Pennsylvania Reserves
6th Pennsylvania Reserves · 13th Pennsylvania Reserves (1st Rifles)
121st Pennsylvania

Second Brigade Col. Albert L. Magilton
3d Pennsylvania Reserves · 4th Pennsylvania Reserves
7th Pennsylvania Reserves · 8th Pennsylvania Reserves
142d Pennsylvania

Third Brigade Brig. Gen. Conrad Feger Jackson;
Col. Joseph W. Fisher; Lieut. Col. Robert Anderson
5th Pennsylvania Reserves · 9th Pennsylvania Reserves
10th Pennsylvania Reserves · 11th Pennsylvania Reserves
12th Pennsylvania Reserves

Artillery
1st Pennsylvania Light, Battery A · 1st Pennsylvania Light, Battery B
1st Pennsylvania Light, Battery G · 5th United States, Battery C

SIXTH ARMY CORPS Maj. Gen. William F. Smith
ESCORT *10th New York Cavalry, Company L*
6th Pennsylvania Cavalry, Company I
6th Pennsylvania Cavalry, Company K

First Division Brig. Gen. William T. H. Brooks
First Brigade Col. Alfred T. A. Torbert
1st New Jersey · 2d New Jersey · 3d New Jersey · 4th New Jersey
15th New Jersey · 23d New Jersey

Second Brigade Col. Henry L. Cake
5th Maine · 16th New York · 27th New York · 121st New York
96th Pennsylvania

Third Brigade Brig. Gen. David A. Russell
18th New York · 31st New York · 32d New York · 95th Pennsylvania

Artillery
Maryland Light, Battery A · Massachusetts Light, 1st Battery (A)
New Jersey Light, 1st Battery · 2d United States, Battery D

SECOND DIVISION Brig. Gen. Albion P. Howe
First Brigade Brig. Gen. Calvin E. Pratt
6th Maine · 43d New York · 49th Pennsylvania · 119th Pennsylvania
5th Wisconsin

Second Brigade Col. Henry Whiting
26th New Jersey · 2d Vermont · 3d Vermont · 4th Vermont
5th Vermont · 6th Vermont

Third Brigade Brig. Gen. Francis L. Vinton;
Col. Robert F. Taylor; Brig. Gen. Thomas H. Neill
21st New Jersey · 20th New York · 33d New York · 49th New York
77th New York

Artillery
Maryland Light, Battery B · New York Light, 1st Battery
New York Light, 3d Battery · 5th United States, Battery F

Third Division Brig. Gen. John Newton
First Brigade Brig. Gen. John Cochrane
65th New York · 67th New York · 122d New York
23d Pennsylvania · 61st Pennsylvania · 82d Pennsylvania

Second Brigade Brig. Gen. Charles Devens, Jr.
7th Massachusetts · 10th Massachusetts · 37th Massachusetts
36th New York · 2d Rhode Island

Third Brigade Col Thomas A. Rowley;
Brig. Gen. Frank Wheaton
62d New York · 93d Pennsylvania · 98th Pennsylvania
102d Pennsylvania · 139th Pennsylvania

Artillery
1st Pennsylvania Light, Battery C · 1st Pennsylvania Light, Battery D
2d United States, Battery G

Cavalry Brigade Brig. Gen. George D. Bayard;
Col. David McM. Gregg
District of Columbia, Independent Company · 1st Maine
1st New Jersey · 2d New York · 10th New York · 1st Pennsylvania

Artillery
3d United States Battery C

* * *

THE ARMY OF NORTHERN VIRGINIA
Gen. Robert E. Lee

FIRST CORPS Lt. Gen. James Longstreet
McLaws' Division Maj. Gen. Lafayette McLaws
Kershaw's Brigade Brigadier General Joseph B. Kershaw
2nd South Carolina · 3rd South Carolina
7th South Carolina · 8th South Carolina
15th South Carolina · 3rd South Carolina Battalion

Barksdale's Brigade Brig. Gen. William Barksdale
13th Mississippi · 17th Mississippi · 18th Mississippi
21st Mississippi

Cobb's Brigade Brig. Gen. T. R. R. Cobb;
Col. Robert McMillan
16th Georgia · 18th Georgia · 24th Georgia · Cobb's (Georgia) Legion
Phillips' (Georgia) Legion

Semmes' Brigade Brig. Gen. Paul J. Semmes
10th Georgia · 50th Georgia · 51st Georgia · 53rd Georgia

Artillery Col. Henry C. Cabell
Manly's (North Carolina) Battery
1st Richmond Howitzers Troup (Georgia) Artillery
Pulaski (Georgia) Artillery · Richmond (Fayette) Artillery

Anderson's Division Maj. Gen. Richard H. Anderson
Wilcox's Brigade Brig. Gen. Cadmus M. Wilcox
8th Alabama · 9th Alabama · 10th Alabama · 11th Alabama
14th Alabama

Featherston's Brigade Brig. Gen. W. S. Featherston
12th Mississippi · 16th Mississippi · 19th Mississippi
48th Mississippi

Mahone's Brigade Brig. Gen. William Mahone
6th Virginia · 12th Virginia · 16th Virginia · 41st Virginia
61st Virginia

Wright's Brigade Brig. Gen. Ambrose R. Wright
3rd Georgia · 22nd Georgia · 48th Georgia · 2nd Georgia Battalion

Perry's Brigade Brig. Gen. E. A. Perry
2nd Florida · 5th Florida · 8th Florida

Artillery
Donaldsonville (Louisiana) Artillery · Huger's (Virginia) Battery
Lewis's (Virginia) Battery · Norfolk (Virginia) Light Artillery Blues

Pickett's Division Maj. Gen. George E. Pickett
Garnett's Brigade Brig. Gen. Richard B. Garnett
8th Virginia · 18th Virginia · 19th Virginia · 28th Virginia
56th Virginia

Kemper's Brigade Brig. Gen. James L. Kemper
1st Virginia · 3rd Virginia · 7th Virginia · 11th Virginia · 24th Virginia

Armistead's Brigade Brig. Gen. Lewis A. Armistead
9th Virginia · 14th Virginia · 38th Virginia · 53rd Virginia
57th Virginia

Jenkins' Brigade Brig. Gen. Micah Jenkins
1st South Carolina · 2nd South Carolina (Rifles) · 5th South Carolina
6th South Carolina · Hampton Legion · Palmetto Sharpshooters

Corse's Brigade Brig. Gen. Montgomery D. Corse
15th Virginia · 17th Virginia · 30th Virginia · 32nd Virginia

Artillery
Dearing's (Virginia) Battery · Fauquier (Virginia) Artillery
Richmond Fayette Artillery

Hood's Division Maj. Gen. John B. Hood
Law's Brigade Brig. Gen. Evander M. Law
4th Alabama · 44th Alabama · 6th North Carolina
54th North Carolina · 57th North Carolina

Anderson's Brigade Brig. Gen. George T. Anderson
1st Georgia (Regulars) · 7th Georgia · 8th Georgia · 9th Georgia
11th Georgia

Robertson's Brigade Brig. Gen. J. B. Robertson
3rd Arkansas · 1st Texas · 4th Texas · 5th Texas

Toombs' Brigade Col. Henry L. Benning
2nd Georgia · 15th Georgia · 17th Georgia · 20th Georgia

Artillery
German (South Carolina) Artillery
Palmetto (South Carolina) Light Artillery
Rowan (North Carolina) Artillery

Ransom's Division Brig. Gen. Robert Ransom, Jr.
Ransom's Brigade Brig. Gen. Robert Ransom, Jr.
24th North Carolina · 25th North Carolina · 35th North Carolina
49th North Carolina · Branch's (Virginia) Battery

Cooke's Brigade Brig. Gen. J. R. Cooke; Col. E. D. Hall
15th North Carolina · 27th North Carolina · 46th North Carolina
48th North Carolina · Cooper's (Virginia) Battery

First Corps Artillery
Washington (Louisiana) Artillery · 1st Company · 2nd Company
3rd Company · 4th Company

Alexander's Battalion Lieut. Col. E. Porter Alexander
Bedford (Virginia) Artillery · Eubank's (Virginia) Battery
Madison Light Artillery (Louisiana) · Parker's (Virginia) Battery
Rhett's (South Carolina) Battery · Woolfolk's (Virginia) Battery

SECOND CORPS Lieut. Gen. Thomas J. Jackson
D. H. Hill's Division Maj. Gen. Daniel H. Hill
First Brigade Brig. Gen. Robert E. Rodes
3rd Alabama · 5th Alabama · 6th Alabama · 12th Alabama
26th Alabama

Second (Ripley's) Brigade Brig. Gen. George Doles
4th Georgia · 44th Georgia · 1st North Carolina · 3rd North Carolina

Third Brigade Brig. Gen. Alfred H. Colquitt
13th Alabama · 6th Georgia · 23rd Georgia · 27th Georgia
28th Georgia

Fourth Brigade Brig. Gen. Alfred Iverson
5th North Carolina · 12th North Carolina · 20th North Carolina
23rd North Carolina

Fifth (Ramseur's) Brigade Col. Bryan Grimes
2nd North Carolina · 4th North Carolina · 14th North Carolina
30th North Carolina

Artillery Maj. H. P. Jones
King William (Virginia) Artillery · Hardaway's (Alabama) Battery
Jeff. Davis (Alabama) Artillery · Morris (Virginia) Artillery
Orange (Virginia) Artillery

A. P. Hill's Division Maj. Gen. Ambrose P. Hill
First (Field's) Brigade Col. J. M. Brockenbrough
40th Virginia · 47th Virginia · 55th Virginia · 22nd Virginia Battalion

Second Brigade Brig. Gen. Maxcy Gregg;
Col. D. H. Hamilton
1st South Carolina Provisional Army · 1st South Carolina Rifles
12th South Carolina · 13th South Carolina · 14th South Carolina

Third Brigade Brig. Gen. E. L. Thomas
14th Georgia · 35th Georgia · 45th Georgia · 49th Georgia

Fourth Brigade Brig. Gen. J. H. Lane
7th North Carolina · 18th North Carolina · 28th North Carolina
33rd North Carolina · 37th North Carolina

Fifth Brigade Brig. Gen. James J. Archer
5th Alabama Battalion · 19th Georgia · 1st Tennessee (Provisional Army)
7th Tennessee · 14th Tennessee

Sixth Brigade Brig. Gen. William D. Pender;
Col. Alfred M. Scales
13th North Carolina · 16th North Carolina · 22nd North Carolina
34th North Carolina · 38th North Carolina

Artillery Lieut. Col. R. L. Walker
Branch (North Carolina) Artillery · Crenshaw (Virginia) Battery
Fredericksburg (Virginia) Artillery · Johnson's (Virginia) Battery
Letcher (Virginia) Artillery · Pee Dee (South Carolina) Artillery
Purcell (Virginia) Artillery

Ewell's Division Brig. Gen. Jubal A. Early
Lawton's Brigade Col. Edmund N. Atkinson;
Col. Clement A. Evans
13th Georgia · 26th Georgia · 31st Georgia · 38th Georgia
60th Georgia · 61st Georgia

Early's Brigade Col. James A. Walker
13th Virginia · 25th Virginia · 31st Virginia · 44th Virginia
49th Virginia · 52nd Virginia · 58th Virginia

Trimble's Brigade Col. Robert F. Hoke
15th Alabama · 12th Georgia · 21st Georgia · 21st North Carolina
1st North Carolina Battalion

Hays' (First Louisiana) Brigade Brig. Gen. Harry T. Hays
5th Louisiana · 6th Louisiana · 7th Louisiana · 8th Louisiana
9th Louisiana

Artillery Capt. J. W. Latimer
Charlottesville (Virginia) · Chesapeake (Maryland) · Courtney (Virginia)
1st Maryland Battery · Louisiana Guard Artillery
Staunton (Virginia) Artillery

Jackson's Division Brig. Gen. William B. Taliaferro
First Brigade Brig. Gen. E. F. Paxton
2nd Virginia · 4th Virginia · 5th Virginia · 27th Virginia
33rd Virginia

Second Brigade Brig. Gen. J. R. Jones
21st Virginia · 42nd Virginia · 48th Virginia · 1st Virginia Battalion

Third (Taliaferro's) Brigade Col. E. T. H. Warren
47th Alabama · 48th Alabama · 10th Virginia · 23rd Virginia
37th Virginia

Fourth (Starke's) Brigade Col. Edmund Pendleton
1st Louisiana (Volunteers) · 2nd Louisiana · 10th Louisiana
14th Louisiana · 15th Louisiana · Coppen's (Louisiana) Battalion

Artillery Capt. J. B. Brockenbrough
Carpenter's (Virginia) Battery · Danville (Virginia) Artillery
Hampden (Virginia) Artillery · Lee (Virginia) Artillery
Lusk's (Virginia) Battery

RESERVE ARTILLERY Brig. Gen. William N. Pendleton
Brown's Battalion Col. J. Thompson Brown
*Salem Artillery, Hupp's Battery · Rockbridge Artillery · Brooke's
(Virginia) Battery · 2nd Richmond (Virginia) Howitzers
3rd Richmond (Virginia) Howitzers · Powhatan (Virginia) Artillery*
Sumter (Georgia) Battalion Lieut. Col. Allen S. Cutts
Company A · Company B · Company C

Nelson's Battalion Maj. William Nelson
*Amherst (Virginia) Artillery · Fluvanna (Virginia) Artillery
Georgia Battery*

Miscellaneous Batteries
Ells' (Georgia) Battery · Hanover Artillery

CAVALRY Maj. Gen. James E. B. Stuart
First Brigade Brig. Gen. Wade Hampton
*1st North Carolina · 1st South Carolina · 2nd South Carolina
Cobb's (Georgia) Legion · Phillips' (Georgia) Legion*

Second Brigade Brig. Gen. Fitzhugh Lee
1st Virginia · 2nd Virginia · 3rd Virginia · 4th Virginia · 5th Virginia

Third Brigade Brig. Gen. W. H. F. Lee
*2nd North Carolina · 9th Virginia · 10th Virginia · 13th Virginia
15th Virginia*

Fourth Brigade Brigadier General William Jones
*6th Virginia Cavalry · 7th Virginia Cavalry · 12th Virginia Cavalry
17th Virginia Battalion Cavalry · 35th Virginia Battalion Cavalry*

Artillery Maj. John Pelham
*Breathed's (Virginia) Battery · Chew's (Virginia) Battery
Hart's (South Carolina) Battery · Henry's (Virginia) Battery
Moorman's (Virginia) Battery*

The Fredericksburg Campaign: Decision on the Rappahannock
Edited by Gary W. Gallagher
The University of North Carolina Press (1995)
ISBN-13: 978-0807858950 (paperback, 2007)

Gallagher's work collects essays from some of the leading authors on the battle: William A. Blair, A. Wilson Greene, William Marvel, Alan Nolan, George Rable, Carol Reardon, and Gallagher himself. For those who know the battle, Gallagher's book provides an excellent collection of essays that explores a variety of topics in detail: Ambrose Burnside and the Union high command, Confederate leadership, the impact of the Union army on civilians, the carnage of the battle, the Mud March, and more.

The Fredericksburg Campaign: Winter War on the Rappahannock
Francis Augustine O'Reilly
Louisiana State University Press (2003)
ISBN-13: 978-0807131541 (paperback, 2006)

Historically, most of the attention on the Battle of Fredericksburg has focused on the tragedy in front of the Stone Wall; few students of the battle considered the role of the fight at the south end of the field. O'Reilly's exhaustive research uncovered new evidence that forced an entire reinterpretation of the battle. The Fredericksburg Campaign is the must-read book for anyone who wants the full understanding of the battle and its inner workings. Utilizing extensive first-hand accounts, O'Reilly crafts a thorough, highly readable microtactical study.

War So Terrible: A Popular History
of the Battle of Fredericksburg
Donald C. Pfanz
Page One History Publications (2003)
ISBN-13: 978-0970436719

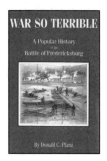

Originally written as a series of newspaper articles, Pfanz's book is an excellent collection of vignettes and human interest stories covering the entire Fredericksburg campaign. For any reader looking for something a bit more in depth than *Simply Murder* without diving into a heavy tome, Pfanz's engaging book offers the perfect answer.

Fredericksburg! Fredericksburg!
George C. Rable
The University of North Carolina Press (2001)
ISBN-13: 978-0807872697 (paperback, 2012)

Rable's valuable study puts the Fredericksburg campaign into a larger context. The book goes from the battlefront to the homefront in a supple blend of political, social, and military history. Adopting a fair, balanced approach, Rable also examines post-battle reactions in the North and the South.

Blood on the Rappahannock:
The Battle of Fredericksburg
Edited by Ted Savas
Civil War Regiments book issue, Vol. 4, No. 4.
Regimental Studies, Inc. (paperback, 1995)

An outstanding collection of original essays on units, personalities, and combat actions that helped shape the course and outcome of the fighting at Fredericksburg. Topics include The assault of the Pennsylvania Reserves, the Death of Confederate General Thomas R. R. Cobb, Private William McCarter and the attack of the Irish Brigade on Marye's Heights, Stonewall Jackson's artillery and the defense of the Confederate right flank, the 20th Massachusetts Infantry and the fight for the streets of Fredericksburg, and more.

About the Authors

Chris Mackowski is a professor in the School of Journalism and Mass Communication at St. Bonaventure University in Allegany, NY. He also works as a historian with the National Park Service at Fredericksburg & Spotsylvania National Military Park, where he gives tours at four major Civil War battlefields (Fredericksburg, Chancellorsville, Wilderness, and Spotsylvania), as well as at the building where Stonewall Jackson died. He's the author of *Chancellorsville: Crossroads of Fire* and *The Dark, Close Wood: The Wilderness, Ellwood, and the Battle that Transformed Both*, and his writing has appeared in several national magazines. He blogs regularly for *Scholars and Rogues* <www.scholarsandrogues.com>.

Kristopher D. White is a historian for the Penn-Trafford Recreation Board and a continuing education instructor for the Community College of Allegheny County near Pittsburgh, PA. White is a graduate of Norwich University with a M.A. in Military History, as well as a graduate of California University of Pennsylvania with a B.A. in History. For five years he served as a staff military historian at Fredericksburg and Spotsylvania National Military Park, where he still volunteers his services. For a short time, he was a member of the Association of Licensed Battlefield Guides at Gettysburg. Over the past seven years, he has spoken to more than thirty roundtables and historical societies.

Chris and **Kris**, longtime friends, have co-authored several books together, including *The Last Days of Stonewall Jackson, Chancellorsville's Forgotten Front: The Battles of Second Fredericksburg and Salem Church*, and *Simply Murder: The Battle of Fredericksburg*, along with monograph-length articles on the battle of Spotsylvania for *Blue & Gray*. Mackowski and White have also written for *Civil War Times, America's Civil War*, and *Hallowed Ground*. They are co-founders of the blog *Emerging Civil War* <www.emergingcivilwar.com>.

EMERGING CIVIL WAR SERIES